Relational
Intelligence

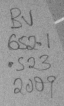

Relational Intelligence

How Leaders Can Expand Their Influence Through a New Way of Being Smart

STEVE SACCONE

FOREWORD BY ERWIN RAPHAEL McMANUS

JOSSEY-BASS
A Wiley Imprint
www.josseybass.com

Published by Jossey-Bass
A Wiley Imprint
989 Market Street, San Francisco, CA 94103-1741—www.josseybass.com

Jossey-Bass books and products are available through most bookstores. To contact Jossey-Bass directly call our Customer Care Department within the U.S. at 800-956-7739, outside the U.S. at 317-572-3986, or fax 317-572-4002.

Jossey-Bass also publishes its books in a variety of electronic formats. Some content that appears in print may not be available in electronic books.

All Scripture attributions are listed in the Notes section at the end of the book.

Scripture quotations marked (NIV) are taken from the HOLY BIBLE, NEW INTERNATIONAL VERSION®. NIV®. Copyright © 1973, 1978, 1984 by International Bible Society. Used by permission of Zondervan. All rights reserved.

Scripture quotations marked (NASB) are taken from the New American Standard Bible®, Copyright © 1960, 1962, 1963, 1968, 1971, 1972, 1973, 1975, 1977, 1995 by The Lockman Foundation. Used by permission. (www.Lockman.org)

Scripture quotations marked (TNIV) are taken from the HOLY BIBLE, TODAY'S NEW INTERNATIONAL VERSION®. TNIV®. Copyright© 2001, 2005 by International Bible Society. Used by permission of Zondervan. All rights reserved.

Scripture taken from The Message. Copyright 1993, 1994, 1995, 1996, 2000, 2001, 2002. Used by permission of NavPress Publishing Group.

Library of Congress Cataloging-in-Publication Data

Saccone, Steve, date.
  Relational intelligence : how leaders can expand their influence through a new way of being smart / Steve Saccone; foreword by Erwin Raphael McManus.—1st ed.
    p. cm.—(Leadership network series)
  Includes bibliographical references and index.
  ISBN 978-0-470-43869-5 (cloth)
    1. Christian leadership. 2. Interpersonal relations—Religious aspects—Christianity. I. Title.
  BV652.1.S23 2009
  253—dc22   2009018598

Printed in the United States of America
FIRST EDITION

HB Printing 10 9 8 7 6 5 4 3 2 1

Leadership Network Titles

The Leader's Journey: Accepting the Call to Personal and Congregational Transformation, Jim Herrington, Robert Creech, and Trisha Taylor

Whole Church: Leading from Fragmentation to Engagement, Mel Lawrenz

Culture Shift: Transforming Your Church from the Inside Out, Robert Lewis and Wayne Cordeiro, with Warren Bird

Church Unique: How Missional Leaders Cast Vision, Capture Culture, and Create Movement, Will Mancini

A New Kind of Christian: A Tale of Two Friends on a Spiritual Journey, Brian D. McLaren

The Story We Find Ourselves In: Further Adventures of a New Kind of Christian, Brian D. McLaren

Missional Renaissance: Changing the Scorecard for the Church, Reggie McNeal

Practicing Greatness: 7 Disciplines of Extraordinary Spiritual Leaders, Reggie McNeal

The Present Future: Six Tough Questions for the Church, Reggie McNeal

A Work of Heart: Understanding How God Shapes Spiritual Leaders, Reggie McNeal

The Millennium Matrix: Reclaiming the Past, Reframing the Future of the Church, M. Rex Miller

Shaped by God's Heart: The Passion and Practices of Missional Churches, Milfred Minatrea

The Missional Leader: Equipping Your Church to Reach a Changing World, Alan J. Roxburgh and Fred Romanuk

Relational Intelligence: How Leaders Can Expand Their Influence Through a New Way of Being Smart, Steve Saccone

The Ascent of a Leader: How Ordinary Relationships Develop Extraordinary Character and Influence, Bill Thrall, Bruce McNicol, and Ken McElrath

Beyond Megachurch Myths: What We Can Learn from America's Largest Churches, Scott Thumma and Dave Travis

The Elephant in the Boardroom: Speaking the Unspoken About Pastoral Transitions, Carolyn Weese and J. Russell Crabtree

Contents

About Leadership Network

Since 1984, Leadership Network has fostered church innovation and growth by diligently pursuing its far-reaching mission statement: to identify, connect, and help high-capacity Christian leaders multiply their impact.

Although Leadership Network's techniques adapt and change as the church faces new opportunities and challenges, the organization's work follows a consistent and proven pattern: Leadership Network brings together entrepreneurial leaders who are focused on similar ministry initiatives. The ensuing collaboration—often across denominational lines—creates a strong base from which individual leaders can better analyze and refine their own strategies. Peer-to-peer interaction, dialogue, and sharing inevitably accelerate participants' innovation and ideas. Leadership Network further enhances this process through developing and distributing highly targeted ministry tools and resources, including audio and video programs, special reports, e-publications, and online downloads.

With Leadership Network's assistance, today's Christian leaders are energized, equipped, inspired, and better able to multiply their own dynamic Kingdom-building initiatives.

Launched in 1996 in conjunction with Jossey-Bass (a Wiley imprint), Leadership Network Publications present thoroughly researched and innovative concepts from leading thinkers, practitioners, and pioneering churches. The series collectively draws from a range of disciplines, with individual titles offering perspective on one or more of five primary areas:

1. Enabling effective leadership
2. Encouraging life-changing service
3. Building authentic community
4. Creating Kingdom-centered impact
5. Engaging cultural and demographic realities

For additional information on the mission or activities of Leadership Network, please contact:

Leadership Network
(800) 765-5323
client.care@leadnet.org

Foreword

I have had the privilege of knowing Steve and his amazing wife, Cheri, for several years now, and I still remember the day we met. They both left an unforgettable impression on my life. They had been recommended by a friend who spoke of them in such glowing terms that I was certain I was being set up for disappointment. My friend was right, and I was more than pleasantly surprised. I knew right away that in a world enamored with high-powered leadership styles and in a culture addicted to style over substance, Steve may be potentially overlooked and underestimated. Steve wasn't the proverbial diamond in the rough; he was a diamond in a world that valued glitter. He wasn't going to grab your attention with how bright he shined; he would, however, illuminate any room with the light he brought out in others. In a strange way, Steve's greatest gifts are the ones he brings out in those who work with him. He has over the years developed an absurd number of leaders, all of whom consider Steve a good friend. This is what I think makes Steve unique and uniquely qualified to write this book. Steve doesn't work with bosses, peers, or subordinates—he works with friends. Regardless of his role or organizational position, relationship is the unifying core of everything he does and everyone he works with. Steve doesn't so much lead through teams as he leads through community. And he does this with great intelligence—specifically relational intelligence.

People come from all over the world to Los Angeles to experience and observe Mosaic. They come hoping to glean a new approach to ministry or to discover what the church will look like in the future. Given only a few hours around one of our gatherings, they might leave inspired by the creativity and artistry of our community, or they might leave determined to reflect our diversity as they see the world come together across seven different locations. Only those who are careful observers will see that what really makes Mosaic possible is a deep investment in people and a profound commitment to being authentically human. It is in this context that Steve rises to the surface. The greatest compliment I could give Steve, and he fully personifies it, is that he is a "true human."

As a leader, Steve not only brings out the best in others as leaders but also brings out their humanity. The great danger lies in becoming a better leader without becoming a better person. Wherever possible, we need to redefine what leadership really is and is not. Great leadership should and must become inseparable from nobility, honor, and virtue and never again be mutually exclusive. Neither can leadership continue down the path of using—I'm sorry, *recruiting*—people to fulfill the leader's vision. Far too many leadership conversations address people as commodities to be distributed and discarded based on the leader's own needs and desires. True leaders are as committed to helping those under their care find their unique path and purpose as they are to fulfilling their own. The basis of Steve's philosophy is that people matter, that they are our greatest resource, and that real leadership requires relational intelligence.

In *Wide Awake*, I focus on eight characteristics of the person who continually lives out his or her greatest dreams. This person is identified by both a description and a hero. I close the book with what I feel is the most critical attribute needed to live our most heroic lives. The chapter is titled "Invest," and the hero is the Romantic. "Invest" offers an observation and an opportunity. The observation is that we can never fulfill our greatest dreams without the goodwill and help of others. Simply put—we need people. The opportunity is to be that person for others. Again in simple terms—people need you. *Relational Intelligence* will elevate both your awareness and perceptivity in regard to both of these dynamics.

o o o

This past year we have, as a team, been practicing the art of awareness. A lifetime of exploration has left me with the discovery that there is a language we humans speak that goes far beyond words. I have spent the last four decades listening to what people are really saying. The more carefully I listened and the more closely I paid attention, the more clearly I could hear what wasn't being said. Language has become secondary to me; communication and understanding, primary. When I was younger, I would say I could see emotions the way others see furniture. Unfortunately, many leaders see the goals clearly, but are visually impaired when it comes to people. If you're ready to leave behind antiquated models of leadership where results rule over relationship, and to join those who are convinced that the future is waiting within the untapped potential of the people they lead, then it's time to increase your relational intelligence. You're going to need it.

Create the future,
Erwin Raphael McManus

Heroes to Acknowledge

The stories of our lives are filled with dreams; some come true, and some do not. When a dream does come true, you stand in awe, wondering how exactly it all happened. For me, the book you are holding is a dream come true, and without so many significant people in my life this would never have become a reality.

In my journey through life, there are heroes who shaped who I've become and what I've accomplished. They are the characters in my story who invested in me, brought out my best, and sacrificed for reasons I don't fully understand. But when God brings these people into your life, you treasure them, and hold them close to your heart because they are so rare. Some of these people have made immense contributions to this book, and for that I am forever grateful.

Cheri, you are without question the most remarkable hero in my life. More than anyone, you've made so many of my dreams become a reality—and this is certainly one of them. Writing this book (together) brought us new challenges, and through them the depth of who you are was once again displayed as the incredible person I know you to be. Willingly, you spent endless hours sharpening my thoughts and ideas, and offering yours freely (they are usually much better than mine). I have never known anyone with such an abundance of relational wisdom and ability to clearly articulate insights. Every step of the way, you immersed yourself in this writing process with unmatched devotion, diligence, and loyalty to me. You gave so much, and I cannot express in words how grateful I am for your sacrifices, generosity, and patience. Your fingerprints are on every page of this book, and I hope you know how deeply grateful I am for your endless devotion to me through this process—it goes beyond what anyone will ever know.

To other heroes in my story:

Sheryl Fullerton: Thank you for your relentless honesty, flexibility, and quality input. Your strengths helped improve my weaknesses and filled gaps that would still be in this book if not for you.

The whole crew at Jossey-Bass and Leadership Network: Thank you for risking greatly and believing in my message. I'm extremely honored to partner with you.

Erwin McManus: You are not only a great leader but also a dream catcher. You see possibilities in people and help them live out dreams they didn't even know existed. You've shifted my paradigms and given me life-changing opportunities; your investment in me has been priceless. There are not enough words to express how thankful I am to you, and this book is a tribute of my gratitude.

Tina Jacobson: I'm deeply indebted to you because this book might not have happened without you. Thanks for representing me so well, and for going above and beyond. I benefited not only from all your years of experience but also from the kindness you showed me along the way.

Daniel Hill: Thank you for your persistent demand for clarity and focus, for your relational wisdom and input, and for the creative energy that emerged from our ongoing conversation through life. Your contributions were so meaningful to me, and I'm deeply grateful for them.

Gary Hill: Thanks for your *energy*, for shaping so much of my theological foundation, and for offering your insights on human relationships as God designed them to be.

David Haley, Michael Muniz, Scot Burbank, Jason Jaggard, Sueann Cho, and Hank Fortener: You went above and beyond to help make this book better chapter by chapter. Thanks for giving so freely and generously; your input mattered more than you know.

Joby Harris: For your creative ideas, for offering yourself so freely, and for your constant spirit of generosity.

Mom and Dad: Thank you for a lifetime of unconditional love, and for teaching me so much about relationships.

And last, words cannot capture my immense gratitude to God, the One who gives so fully and undeservingly. Writing has been an incredible privilege and an extraordinary act of grace that has filled my heart with joy and worship. Most of all: God, I pray this book honors You.

Relational Intelligence

PART
1

The Origins of Relational Intelligence

Human relationships are often reduced to a commodity, as if people were buying, selling, and trading them for their own good. People often value relationships for the wrong reasons. Perhaps it is because a relationship helps them feel empowered in a world where they feel powerless, or because it can help them receive a significant promotion in their field of work; sometimes relationships can be useful for people as they seek to advance their own ambition or feed their own narcissism. When we value relationships for the wrong reasons, or when there is no advantage to be gained, people quickly become disposable. But relationships must not be reduced to a commodity and must not be disposable, because they are God's highest value and intersect the essence of what it means to be human. The way we choose to relate to one another defines the quality of our human experience and reveals what we value most. This is where the journey of relational intelligence begins.

At the intersection of intelligence and relationships is a man who completely embodies the synergy of both. Jesus is that man. He was the most relationally intelligent person who ever walked this Earth. He compelled people to Himself through authentic love and compassion. He accepted people where they were at, while at the same time challenging them to grow and change. He extended grace, but also carried out justice. He related to people with confidence while simultaneously remaining humble. He knew when to challenge others and when to encourage them. On His brief journey when He walked on Earth, He never saw a single person as disposable or unworthy. He was highly relational and knew how to consistently guide people wisely and meaningfully. If we explore the relational world in the life of Jesus, and if we really absorb how He approached leadership, we discover His emphasis on the quality of relationship.

As leaders, we tend to focus more on quantity than quality, but Jesus' approach to leadership was different. This may be most clearly seen in how He related to and invested in His twelve disciples. He never skimped on the *quality*, and what followed was an enormous *quantity* of influence, which continues to have far-reaching effects today. The longer I am in leadership, the more I learn that bigger is not always better, that faster doesn't always get us where we want to go, and that quantity ought to be a by-product of quality rather than an end in itself.

Relational Intelligence strives to guide leaders in reprioritizing their emphasis on the quality in their relationships, and in doing so expand their ability to influence others more effectively. This doesn't mean we should eliminate the pursuit of quantity altogether; it simply means that quality must precede quantity if we want our influence to be deeply and personally transformational for others. Who knows? Maybe applying this new way of being smart will accelerate the far-reaching effects of your impact in ways you could never imagine, while at the same time making you and me better human beings.

The Human Economy

Man is a knot into which relationships are tied.
—*Antoine de Saint-Exupéry,*
Flight to Arras

Although Carly and I had been in eighth grade together, something changed when I saw her in ninth grade. When she walked into the room, it seemed that every teenage boy had his eye on the girl I thought was the prettiest one at school. But there was a big obstacle to asking her out: her beauty intimidated me.

After a couple months, I stopped allowing my fear of rejection to stifle my pursuit. I devised a scheme to ask her out that guaranteed a response of yes. It was a simple strategy, one that many others use when they're young and infatuated (and even when they are adult men with perceived courage and strength). I decided to ask her friends if she "liked me," while ensuring that she wouldn't find out that I *liked her*. To my surprise, I discovered Carly had a little thing for me as well!

She agreed to go out with me, but for fourteen-year-olds, what is dating anyway? I wasn't even old enough to drive. The only money I had was from my parents for taking out the trash and washing dishes. For me, dating involved seeing each other at lunch and at our lockers between classes. Of course we also talked on the phone at night, which was often filled with uncomfortable silence. But isn't awkwardness the teenage modus operandi? I decided to move forward anyway.

Two weeks into our "dating relationship," I took Carly on our first date. That is, I asked to see if her mom could drop her off at my house on Friday night—and she did. After she met my parents, they went into the next room and left us by ourselves. I was nervous about whether we could make conversation for two hours; after all, I was a teenage boy used to having entire conversations consisting of grunts and comments on bodily functions. But in an effort to avoid this dilemma, I had rented a romantic comedy. After the movie, I was hoping we would have only a few minutes before her mom came; although I really liked her, I didn't know what to talk about. But I tried.

"How did you like the movie?" I asked.

"It was good. How did you like it?"

"I thought it was good too."

That's about the extent of the conversation.

As we sat on my couch, I wanted to connect so badly, but didn't really know how. So I came up with a seemingly brilliant solution. I decided to take our relationship to the next level. I slowly put my arm around her and started rubbing her shoulder. Then my clammy palm grasped hers as I looked into her big brown eyes and attempted to create a meaningful moment. The next thing that came tumbling out of my mouth was, "I love you."

Pure silence.

She just sat there looking at me with a blank stare. It was not so much the look of affection and adoration I was hoping for, but more the look of someone standing in the middle of the road about to get hit by a Mack truck. Saying, "I love you" in that moment was the verbal equivalent of someone jamming a stick into my bike spokes while going thirty miles per hour.

After what seemed like an eternity, Carly managed to get out two words, a confused "Thank you?" Of course she had no idea how to respond. What else could she say? It's no surprise that our relationship ended shortly thereafter. In an effort to take our relationship to the next level, I had said something completely foolish, and it produced the opposite effect from what I wanted. Instead of bringing us closer, it broke us apart.

I didn't know a name for what happened, but the fact is, I didn't have any *relational intelligence*. I tried to create a meaningful moment without doing the work of cultivating the relationship. I attempted to force something that the relationship wasn't ready for. My motives were selfish, and my awareness of her emotions and own desires was not even considered. Not to mention that my approach was awkward, insensitive, and foolish.

My lack of relational intelligence in that moment reflects a bigger reality that has a profound impact on leadership, for better or worse. As leaders, our capacity for relational intelligence can be the cause of both our failures and our successes. One mistake can do enough damage to dissolve a relationship. In one instant, we can destroy what's taken years to build. If you have experienced what it feels like to be the victim of someone else's lack of relational intelligence, you know exactly what I mean. For instance, instead of trying to resolve conflict appropriately, maybe someone verbally attacks you, and as a result your relationship implodes. Or maybe someone makes you believe that he or she is trustworthy, but then violates that trust and wounds you deeply with harsh or inappropriate words. Or maybe you follow someone's leadership because you believed in the person, but when you needed him most he abandons you and leaves you to

> As leaders, our capacity for relational intelligence can be the cause of both our failures and our successes.

fend for yourself, thus breaking up your relationship. In contrast, a person with a high level of relational intelligence knows how to resolve conflict in a healthy manner that fosters the strength of a relationship rather than breaking it down; she earns your trust and is able to sustain it by being a person of integrity and love, and she appreciates your faithfulness to her and in turn is faithful to you when you need her.

As leaders, our intentions are often sincere in wanting to help people move forward, or take a team or group to the next level. But sometimes we don't know exactly how to accomplish our goal. We want to create meaningful moments, but we sometimes end up saying or doing the wrong thing, even when our intentions are good and sincere. As we push people to make progress and pursue a greater purpose, sometimes we find that we're too impatient to do the work of cultivating the relationship that will help them succeed. As leaders, we can sometimes see relationships as simply a means to an end, and this inevitably short-circuits the process needed to apply and implement relational intelligence in our everyday lives and leadership.

What if cultivating smarter relationships became a more integral part of how we approach leading others? What if we focus on the quality of our relationships, which sometimes can be the harder way, but trust that this is also the better way? What if we learn how to create meaningful moments more effectively with others by engaging relational dynamics differently than we have previously done, building trust and credibility that lasts? Our ability to forge healthy relationships is increasingly critical to our leadership effectiveness. In the past, authority and credibility were built on status, power, or position, but in today's world it's built on relationship and trust. To be relationally intelligent, we must shift from a *positional authority mind-set* to the crucial leadership mind-set of *relational authority*. If we want to move forward in expanding our influence, we must ensure that the foundation of relational intelligence is built. And then we'll be on our way toward cultivating a new way of being smart.

Relationships Are the Human Economy

When we hear the word *economy*, we think in terms of finances. The way economics breaks down involves how we spend, invest, and give away our money. But a lot of people would admit that they don't spend adequate time and attention improving the way they handle their finances, which affects their financial intelligence. Whether we neglect or expand our efforts in this arena, we all influence the global economy in some way. And just as the global economy is all about money, the human economy is all about relationships.

Relationships have a direct correlation to the quality of our lives. Unfortunately, many of us often give less-than-optimal effort, focus, and intentionality to maximizing how we spend, invest, and give in our relationships. Wouldn't life be different, and better, if people avoided spending years in the same relationally dysfunctional cycles—at home, at work, or as leaders? What would change if people paid closer attention to how they spend, invest, and give in their relational sphere? What if people kept striving to improve their interaction with others so the quality of their lives would be enhanced and their influence would be expanded?

Because the human economy revolves around relationships, how we choose to spend, invest, and give our lives is of primary importance. Relationships define what it means to be human, which makes them both complicated and fragile. They are the most challenging and complex arena of our lives. They can create enormous amounts of pain, but they can also be the source of indescribable joy. Without relationships, human beings experience loneliness, emptiness, and despair, but when relationships are a present and active part of daily life they give a sense of belonging, fulfillment, and hope. They're critical to our personal well-being and the wholeness of our emotional world,

> Relationships define what it means to be human.

and they even affect our physical health. Relationships are the context from which we find meaning and discover what lasting contributions we can make in the lives of others. Our day-to-day human interactions will determine the quality of our lives more than the tasks or work we do, whether it's in our careers, in leadership, or in any other arena of life. We cannot overestimate the profound effect relationships have on our lives.

Once I was facing a major life decision where the relational connection superseded all other factors in my decision-making process. Upon graduating with my master's degree, I began looking for a job. I found one of great interest in Seattle, and the organization flew me in for an interview. On paper, the job had everything I wanted: it was in a city where Cheri and I both desired to live, a job with an impressive and friendly staff of potential coworkers, a salary much higher than I expected (not to mention a significant spending budget), and then there was a large office they offered to design in any way I wanted. After seven years of school (college and graduate school), including a three-year internship that I actually paid the organization to be part of, this job was looking pretty good.

However, there was one critical missing component. I was unable to establish a relational connection with the person who would ultimately be my boss. It wasn't that he did anything wrong or that he treated me poorly, but after walking away from our interactions with him, Cheri and I felt that there was no potential for the strong relationship that I would need if I were to follow his vision. Although he offered me the job, and although it was a difficult decision in part because it had so many great opportunities I was looking for, I turned it down simply because there was a lack of relational connection.

Shortly afterward, and in direct contrast to that experience, I met the man who is now my boss. Cheri and I were living in Chicago when we met Erwin McManus through our mutual friend Greg. He graciously agreed to meet with us and talk about the possibilities of how we could be a part of Mosaic, the spiritual community he led in Los Angeles. From the moment we met him, we felt an immediate connection with him. That connection continued to grow stronger over the next few hours as we talked and dreamed together about the future. Erwin had made it clear before we met, and even during our meeting, that Mosaic didn't hire people who were not already an integral part of the Mosaic community in Los Angeles. Therefore it wasn't a meeting that was going to result in obtaining a job, but this didn't ultimately dissuade me from my decision. Thanks to the strong relationship established that evening, a job opportunity wasn't even part of my decision-making process. That night, Cheri and I were compelled to the decision to move from Chicago to Los Angeles so that we could become part of this amazing spiritual community, as volunteers. We chose to figure out the rest of the details along the way. Mosaic did hire me later, but after many months of serving and building strong relationships. Today, I have the honor of still working on staff at Mosaic, and it all traces back to establishing a strong relational connection.

In contrast to the first job interview, this option offered nothing initially I was looking for in terms of my career, and there was certainly not any kind of financial benefit. But we had met a leader we believed in, who had a vision we were compelled to support. I wasn't offered a job, but this leader did take the time to meet with me, invest in me, and inspire me. The relationship we established was the much more important thing that persuaded us. Cheri and I made a huge life decision, not based on money, a career opportunity, or the easiest road, but rather on something much less tangible though much more powerful: a relationship. People will ultimately be disappointed with wealth, status, and success alone, but people will thrive and be influenced by the substance and profound nature of their relationships.

It's hard to find anything that matters more than relationships. To understand the full gravity of the power and significance of relationships, we have to look at the origin and source of them. Relationships didn't begin as a human initiative, but instead as a divine one flowing from the center of who God is. God didn't create human beings because He somehow needed us; rather, He created human beings as relational because He exists as a relational being. His desire for us is to enjoy the kind of community that He experiences within Himself. God is not a lonely being searching to find community, because He has community within Himself (Father, Son, and Spirit). Although I cannot comprehend this mystery of how God exists in this capacity, I do know that human beings have been created in His image and likeness, which involves being created as relational beings. What matters most to God is relationships, and that's why they are the foundation of the human economy.

Relationships Are the Virus of Influence

The next foundational element of relational intelligence involves the dynamics of influence, which compares to how viruses infect our immune system. A virus is an infectious agent that reproduces or grows only when it has a host cell or carrier. It can be a bad thing or a good thing. A vaccination can be good when it is a virus injected into our bloodstream to strengthen our immune system. But a bad virus is one that is harmful and breaks down the immune system, making us more vulnerable to disease and illness. When it comes to relational intelligence, we as human beings are all carriers, or host cells. We carry the *virus of influence*, which is called relationship.

> We carry the *virus of influence*, which is called relationship.

As carriers of the virus, we transmit our influence through our human-to-human interactions—for better or worse. And although this viral reality is true for everybody, it has heightened importance for leaders because they carry the virus of influence with stronger intensity and are even more contagious because of their greater capacity to affect others. When leaders embrace the powerful force of this virus, it can empower them to create positive change and a better world through their relationships.

Leaders have the potential to infect people in a way that moves them forward or backward—and this happens primarily through relationship. They can pull people away from what is good, or push them toward it. They have the capacity to strengthen people, or harm them. It can be used to destroy and diminish followers, or to bring life and propel people forward. This dynamic is also what makes influence so dangerous in leadership.

The virus of influence encompasses many things, but its most potent effect is discovered in the spiritual realm. This is both an extraordinary gift and an immense responsibility. Because we human beings are innately spiritual, when we choose to lead we must know that the core of who we are will have a contagious effect on people—for better or worse. Without question, our own spiritual health will spread to those who choose to follow us. True spiritual leaders create relational health around them because they know that their influence flows best wherever healthy relationships exist.

I have a friend who exemplifies true spiritual leadership through relationship. Her name is Sunneye and she works as a teacher in Los Angeles. She's chosen to cultivate relationships with international students on her campus in order to offer friendship to many who are in need, and spiritual guidance to those searching for God. She hosts weekly dinners where she invites students to eat together, get to know one another, and share in intentional discussion groups. Sunneye has affected many people's lives through the gift of relationship—and especially affected one in particular.

Sagar moved to L.A. from India to attend college, and although he loved the experience of moving to a city like L.A. and obtaining an education here, he found himself struggling with the significant changes that come with such a transition. So when Sunneye invited him to dinner with the group, he was immediately drawn to being part of this community, despite not really knowing what it was all about. The friendships in a lonely season of his life compelled him.

On finding out Sunneye was a follower of Jesus, and that she was encouraging spiritual discussion, Sagar was naturally hesitant because he was a devout Hindu. However, because of the kind of person she was, and how Sunneye offered such great friendship to him, he openly engaged in the discussions. In short time, he opened his heart and mind to a God he never knew, and in ways he never imagined he would. Sunneye invited Sagar to Mosaic, but he came initially because she had become a dear friend and he didn't want to offend her. To his surprise, Sagar liked Mosaic and found himself strangely drawn to what he then called "the Mosaic God." This is where a new chapter in his spiritual journey began.

As a result of Sunneye offering her relational space to share with someone she didn't even know, Sagar connected to our faith community. This is where Sagar's journey and mine intersected. We began a friendship, and with it Sagar leaned into his spiritual curiosity. He began asking thought-provoking questions about this "Mosaic God," and even about Jesus.

Because Sagar didn't have a car, I offered to give him a ride to Mosaic, which began our ongoing weekly ritual on Sundays. Our friendship deepened and our conversation about spirituality continued. After several weeks of driving together and talking, Sagar came to a decision. He didn't want to abandon his Hindu religion, but he was ready to make the Mosaic God one of his gods. When I asked him how he came to this decision, he said he could see the effects of this God in Sunneye's life and mine. He noticed how this God opened our hearts to friendship with him and began using us to change his life for the better. He shared with me that he saw the goodness of God in us.

As weeks progressed, I could see Sagar's heart opening more and more to the possibility that Jesus could be real. It's as if I could see him week after week changing little by little.

One Sunday came, like any other, as we drove and attended together, but although this Sunday appeared like the others it was altogether different. On this week, I could see Sagar across the courtyard after the gathering, looking intently for me, with a sense of urgency in his step. He spotted me and moved toward me. I could see his eyes welling up with tears. When we met, he looked at me with the most clarity I'd ever seen in his eyes. I knew I didn't have to say anything, so I just waited for him to speak. When he did, he said, "I no longer want to make the Mosaic God one of my gods. What I want is to make Jesus my one and only God." I could tell he was looking at me for guidance on what to do next, now that he made this declaration out loud. I asked him, "Have you told Jesus what you just told me?" And he said, "No; how do I do that?" Right then we prayed together, and Sagar made Jesus his one and only God.

It never ceases to amaze me how a meaningful relationship can open a person's heart to new spiritual realities never thought possible. Through something as simple as friendship, a person can make decisions that change the trajectory of an entire life. Intelligent relationships are the key that opens the door to humanity's heart, to true spiritual influence. The relationships we build have a viral effect on humanity and will have a direct impact in our leadership.

> Intelligent relationships are the key that opens the door to humanity's heart, to true spiritual influence.

Relationships Are the Proof of God

There's a moment in the Scriptures when Jesus engages the most critical human conversation. He tells his followers that He will be leaving the Earth, and that they will not be able to go where He is going. On numerous occasions, Jesus boils all of life down to one thing: "A new command I give you: love one another."[1] That's a clear, simple marching order, and as the most influential leader in the history of the world Jesus lived it out completely.

Jesus desires to move this value deeper into every human heart and see it expressed through the lives of leaders and in the lives of those they lead. Through the life of Jesus, we can discover the undeniable reality of the primal essence of leadership and the most powerful force of influence: *love*. God chooses to reveal Himself through extraordinary, as well as ordinary, acts of love.

This is not love as we often think of it, as soft, sentimental, or romantic. It's love that is less like the infatuation between Jack and Rose on the *Titanic* and closer to the sacrifice of Oskar Schindler, who risked his own life to rescue thousands from death. When Jesus talked about love, it was alive and real, and it had a transforming effect on people's lives. In fact, there's nothing as fierce and profound as the love that Jesus both embodied and continues to extend to humanity. This love is not like a quiet pond that we easily overpower, but instead a rushing river that is stronger than we can contain. It could be compared to a waterfall that pours down with such force that it has the power to generate enormous amounts of electricity.

Love like this comes with the profound action of serving, risking, and even sacrificing when necessary—all for the sake of others. Jesus often reminds his followers that by this action-oriented and sacrificial love, all humanity will know that they are His followers. God could have chosen a different way to prove Himself. He could have decided to give us extraordinary powers to heal the sick or help the paralyzed walk. He could have given us the ability to bring sight to the blind, or even given us the ability to coerce people to believe in God. He could have told us how to become superhuman in our talent or intellect. But instead of teaching us to be the loudest with our voices, Jesus invited us to be abundantly free with our love. He didn't admonish us to dominate with power, but to bend a knee and serve others. He didn't indulge the part of us that wants to rule, but instead appealed to our hearts and invited us to love well. He didn't command us to force our opinion of truth on others, but to live out His truth with love in our lives. When we follow this way of love, we can become branches outstretched to all of humanity that offers an abundance of goodness and grace.

Jesus told us that *love would be our unifying theme of humanity*, and the powerful reflection of who He is. He created us as relational beings, designed to love one another so that in a human way of love His divine love would mysteriously change us and His love would then be revealed to others. Love is who God created us to become so the world would see and know Him through us. When we love people well, we become the proof of God.

In our attempt to love others, we easily fall prey to loving ourselves too much and loving others too little. Even if we have all the best intentions to love someone, we often end up falling short in expressing it. My hope is that this book can help guide us in overcoming our human shortcomings so we can begin to live out this fierce and powerful love in and through our relationships, so that ultimately people will experience God's love *in them* through our love *for them*.

God will continue to push humanity toward the transformation of our relational worlds, toward expanding our capacity to internalize His love so that we can externalize it to others. God desires to bring us into relationship with Him and into community with one another so that He can reveal to the world the proof of who He is. He wants us to reflect His beauty, brilliance, and wonder, where people begin to see the strength and truth of His character. He intentionally made this possible through the opportunities we're given with people in our daily lives. *Love is the greatest, wisest investment we can make in the human economy*, and if we want to improve our spending habits in love, and learn how to invest in ways that have greater return, we must actualize this love in our relationships. *Relational Intelligence* is a guide to help enhance our ability to do just that, and in turn create a different and better future for the world as we know it. As we move forward, we must keep

> Love is the greatest, wisest investment we can make in the human economy.

the foundation of relationships and influence in mind. But now, let's turn to what *Relational Intelligence* is.

What Is Relational Intelligence?

Most people intuitively know how to define cognitive intelligence. We use such terms as *smart, brilliant,* or *clever.* But even though most of us understand cognitive intelligence at a fundamental level, there's still not a universally agreed-on definition. However, one simple way to define it is as the ability to learn, understand, and comprehend knowledge. Despite our basic understanding, though, there are many more nuances to comprehending the fullness of what it means.

Relational intelligence draws on a similar tension. At a fundamental level, we may intuitively understand what it means, but as we move forward, here's our formal working definition:

> Relational intelligence is the ability to learn, understand, and comprehend knowledge as it relates to interpersonal dynamics.

This definition is the foundational framework to begin learning more about developing our relational potential and expanding our capacity to implement relational intelligence to our leadership. In essence, the purpose of relational intelligence is to enhance the quality of our relationships and expand our influence. We'll continue to expand on the nuanced meaning of relational intelligence, but this book focuses on helping people increase their ability to apply relational intelligence to their leadership and to every aspect of their lives. The goal is not just learning or comprehending knowledge about relationships, but guiding people in advancing their ability to influence through *application* of relational intelligence.

Pursuing relational intelligence (which I'll also begin referring to as RI) is a discovery process that requires our attention, focus, and intentionality if we desire to grow in it. To improve in this arena, we must develop the ability to see into new dimensions of interpersonal dynamics and become smarter in our responses and applications of RI with others. By cultivating RI, we can enhance our ability to affect the people around us more positively. The more relationally intelligent we become, the more we will demonstrate increased love, respect, and trust in every relationship in our lives, which will inevitably elevate our influence.

Measuring Relational Intelligence

Just as an intelligence assessment yields a measurement or score of our cognitive intelligence (IQ = intelligence quotient), a relational assessment measures our relational intelligence and yields our RQ score (RQ = relational quotient). This measures the intelligence of our relationships. You've most likely never taken a relational assessment (or even heard of one), but maybe you took an intelligence assessment when you were young to discover your IQ score. Most experts in the field of cognitive intelligence tell us that a minimal amount of change happens to a person's IQ after the teenage years. This is why, if you took your IQ score at a young age and then also took it later in life, the scores probably came out almost identical. But it could be much different if you did the same thing with your RQ score. Your RQ score can always change.

> Relational intelligence is a *hybrid* of developing social skills and cultivating relational health.

In essence, relational intelligence is a *hybrid* of developing social skills and cultivating relational health. All of us can continue to develop in relational intelligence as we learn from our experiences and interactions with people, as we improve social skills, and as we discover how to cultivate relational health. It is possible to improve in these competencies and grow more adept at navigating our interpersonal interactions and conversations.

Knowing your RQ score can be one gauge to help reveal how well you're learning and applying your knowledge in relationships. If you would like to know your RQ score, go to www.relationalintelligence.info to take an assessment. Then, as you strive to increase your RI, later you can take it again to assess your improvement and growth. It's also helpful to get other people's perspective on your RI in both strengths and weaknesses. Your RQ measures not just your knowledge of relationships but how well you understand and engage in relational dynamics. It can help you see where you need improvement when it comes to cultivating relational health or developing social skills. The results can even uncover how much focus, concentration, and effort you give or don't give to your human relations. In contrast to your IQ score, there's no doubt that your RQ score can be improved as you increase your relational intelligence.

There are many ways to increase our RI: improving how we make decisions, how we interact with others, how we handle conflict or build teams. For instance, let's say a leader is about to begin a team meeting. If she decides to take the path of intentionally developing RI, she approaches this meeting differently than she normally would. She first assesses how her own strengths or weaknesses affect the existing team dynamics. Then this team leader assesses how this intersects the purpose of the team, the strengths and weaknesses of the members, and the personality types and passions of each individual.

RI happens when a person understands that each piece matters and he knows how to put together the puzzle in a way that actualizes his potential as a leader as well as the potential of the team. Just as a person completes a puzzle piece-by-piece, this is what someone with RI does as he develops and applies RI to a given situation. He can assess his relationships piece-by-piece and create a complete picture so as to best accomplish the goal and ultimately increase influence.

Taking the RI approach radically changes how this meeting goes. It affects the beginning (how the leader approaches the situation), the middle (how the leader engages the meeting), and the end (how the leader guides the team toward the best outcome). As a result of this approach, the leader is more centered, self-aware, and fully present in the meeting. During the meeting, each individual also feels more valued, understood, and affirmed. The team members are more connected to one another and more focused on their responsibilities and team goals. The team members become more motivated by enjoying themselves, and feel validated in who they are and in what contributions they can make. Finally, the team members may even begin to have increased respect for the team leader, therefore increasing the leader's ability to influence. All of this is a result of applying RI.

As we move forward, we'll continue to dialogue about how to develop RI as it relates to increasing your self-awareness, cultivating the hidden relational genius with you, maximizing your impact in conversation, learning to create a healthier team culture, and much more. As we travel together through the pages of this book, we're going to develop a multilayered perspective on developing the RI that we desire in our lives, as well as gain insight to help guide others in their journey of RI. We'll also move toward better understanding our RQ score (the measurement of how smart we are in our relationships), beginning with the online assessment tool (www.relationalintelligence.info). In addition, we'll continue to zero in on how our RI affects the dynamics of leadership, influence, and the quality of life in the people around us. Just as someone who studies and observes the brain can gain a more thorough understanding of the deeper dimensions of cognitive intelligence, my hope is that our reading, reflections, and observations throughout this book will give us a more complete and holistic understanding of the deeper dimensions of relational intelligence.

Changing the Future

The best leaders strive to move people on a journey into a different and better future. They peer over the horizon and harness their relationships to pull others forward with them. They are driven to bring change right now so that it changes what could be tomorrow. On this journey, one of their greatest challenges is that they often want to guide people to places they themselves have never even been before. Though there is no GPS (global positioning system) that tells them how to get there, they continue to engage in relationships that build trust and compel people forward, despite their uncertainty about what lies ahead, despite not always knowing the results or outcomes. Leaders realize that the more people they bring with them, the more powerful the effect they can have on changing the future, and making the world a better place. Catalyzing transformational change for the future must be driven through relationships.

∘ ∘ ∘

Relationally intelligent leaders understand at a deep level that they live in a world where relationships are the primary portal through which true change happens. So they strive to cultivate healthy relationships. RI leaders understand that, as much as anyone, leaders are primarily responsible for creating an environment that fosters change in our world, and that the best mode of influence comes when we recognize the intrinsic value of human beings who have been created in the image and likeness of God. Relationships can be demanding, fragile, and complex, and that's why this journey will require our unwavering diligence, determination, wisdom, and intentionality. We know building healthier, better, more influential relationships involves commitment and sacrifice, but if we step forward as leaders then the world around us will ultimately become a more human place that is filled with authentic love.

The Michael
Scott Syndrome

The real voyage of discovery lies not in seeking
new landscapes but in seeing with new eyes.
—Marcel Proust, *In Search of Lost Time*

Have you seen an episode of the TV show *The Office*? It's a comical mockumentary revolving around Michael Scott (the main character, who is played by Steve Carell). He's the manager of a small, and increasingly struggling, fictitious paper company called Dunder Mifflin. One reason his character is so entertaining to watch is that he unknowingly embodies the leader who remains completely unaware of his own contradictory philosophies, offensive insecurities, and oblivious way of constantly insulting people. He's relationally awkward in dealing with his employees and remains blind to any and all of his limitations. Although he's awkwardly and obnoxiously funny, he is mostly naïve in his motives, and he projects

5

his underdeveloped self-awareness into the culture of his work environment and personal life, which produces frequent laughter from his TV audience. (If you haven't seen *The Office*, you're missing the best comedy on TV.)

Michael Scott represents the stereotypical supervisor who has no idea how his employers and friends view him. He's blind to his own dysfunctions, and completely unaware of all the contradictions in his leadership philosophy and practices. His inconsistencies are obvious to everyone, except of course himself. In one episode, he is interviewing for a job and is asked to list his strengths and weaknesses. (Don't you love this question in an interview?)

Michael tells the interviewer that he works harder than he should; he cares more than he ought, and he invests too much time and effort into his work. The interviewer looks puzzled and then asks Michael to tell him what his strengths are. With annoyance in his voice, Michael tells the interviewer, Oh don't you see? My weaknesses and my strengths are the same.

This scene reveals how he views himself—and isn't it like the way we sometimes view ourselves as well? We don't acknowledge our weaknesses, usually because we don't even realize what they are or because we prefer trying to hide them from others. Over and over again, Michael demonstrates complete unawareness about any of his limitations, not to mention having no sense of how others view him.

When someone lacks self-awareness, I refer to this dynamic as the Michael Scott Syndrome, because Michael is the epitome of *self-UNawareness*. Unfortunately, his prognosis is not good because he isn't actively seeking a cure for his syndrome. Instead, he embodies the mantra "ignorance is bliss." As a result, he remains blind to the reality of his relational world, and his leadership attempts suffer greatly. All along, the truth about him is painfully obvious to everyone else.

Even though *The Office* exaggerates these dynamics for the sake of comedy, it does illustrate how lack of self-awareness is one of the most prominent obstacles to RI. We all could probably name a few people who have the syndrome, whether we see them at work, in our personal lives, or in other leadership arenas. Maybe it's that boss who always stereotypes people, but doesn't even realize it—and it's always offensive and insensitive. Or maybe it's a coworker who doesn't realize how irresponsible he or she is but always talks about how other people are being irresponsible.

The truth is, every one of us creates a certain relational culture around us that can have a negative or positive effect. Like Michael, we inject our personality, our value system, our emotions, and whatever our own level of relational *unintelligence* is into these contexts. The more we lack self-awareness, the more potential there is to create a negative environment where we constantly offend people because we don't understand their point of view, or we hurt people's feelings regularly because we lack sensitivity to what they're going through. Our inability to see our own limitations will stifle our ability to build and establish smart relationships.

> Our inability to see our own limitations will stifle our ability to build and establish smart relationships.

It may not surprise you to know that the Michael Scott Syndrome (MSS) is an epidemic. In fact, in my (not exactly) in-depth, formal, and scientific research, I've discovered that ten out of ten people are afflicted with some degree of MSS. No one can escape the contagious effects of this disease—not even you. The temptation is to notice this illness in others but fail to take an honest look at yourself. MSS is a syndrome we all must face. When we sit on the outside looking in, believing we are unaffected by this syndrome, we keep our own relational intelligence from growing. If we stay on the outside, others will be able to see our flaws, but we'll never step forward to identify and overcome them. The truth is, we all have a little bit of Michael Scott in us. If we want to be cured from the syndrome, we need to move from the comfortable idea of ignorance being bliss toward engaging the life-changing reality of self-awareness . . . with honesty, vulnerability, and courage.

An Inside Look

Many leadership gurus, spiritual sages, and people of great influence zero in on the far-reaching effects that lack of awareness can have on people's relationships with one another. Jesus himself addressed this issue of lacking self-awareness in Matthew 7. In this encounter in the Scriptures, a group of people gather around to listen to Him teach. Toward the end of what some call the Sermon on the Mount, He offers advice about the danger of personal dishonesty and pride when it comes to how we tend to deal with our own blind spot:

> Jesus said to a crowd of people, "Why do you look at the speck of sawdust in your brother's eye and pay no attention to the log that is in your own eye? Or how can you say to your brother, 'Let me take the speck of sawdust out of your eye,' and all along there is a log in your own eye?" You hypocrite, first take the log out of your own eye, and then you will see clearly to remove the speck from your brother's eye."[1]

In this teaching, Jesus addresses the instinctive human drift toward comparison, hypocrisy, and arrogance, toward looking at others with a more critical eye than we use for ourselves. He knew that we only loosely hold ourselves to the standards we so dogmatically enforce for others. When we focus our critical attention on others, we tend to become judgmental, proud, and hypocritical. This is why he emphasized looking critically at our

> Our inherent challenge is that we're acutely attuned to dysfunction when we see it in others, but significantly slower to recognize it in ourselves.

own life first before pointing out the deficits of others. He knew that most people, no matter how mature they perceive themselves to be, consistently fail to take a humble and honest look at themselves. Our inherent challenge is that we're acutely attuned to dysfunction when we see it in others, but significantly slower to recognize it in ourselves. We move toward making judgments of the people around us before turning that judgment inward. And sometimes we don't stop there. For a variety of reasons, we may even exaggerate the flaws of others, while minimizing our own.

I certainly am guilty of minimizing my own flaws and magnifying those of others. Sometimes I find myself talking negatively and critically about a mistake that a friend made even though I've made the same mistake many times. When I spot something another person did poorly, I sometimes want to tell someone else about it to make myself feel better about me. If I think someone doesn't tell the whole truth, I want to think of her as a liar because it makes me feel nobler. If someone gives a good talk, I may try to find one thing he didn't do well and tell other people who ask me about it, to put him down and lift myself up.

However this plays out in my life, it's often fueled by my own insecurities and selfishness. It can come from a variety of unhealthy motives, a dysfunctional competitiveness that creeps into my spirit. It may also derive from jealousy or envy, or it can even be pure arrogance, as if I think I'm somehow better than others. Whatever fuels it on a particular day, I know it's a flawed part of me, while it's also revealing of my own skewed perspective. Not only that, I know it can damage a relationship I have with someone if I don't monitor these motives and keep them in check. I'd like to say that I'm always positive about people, and that I don't struggle with insecurity, jealousy, or arrogance. But in the moments that I'm not proud of, I find myself zeroing in on the speck in someone else's eye while ignoring the log in my own.

Work in Progress

When we engage the quest for self-awareness, we're reminded of our humanity—in both our beauty and our brokenness. Knowing our limitations ought not to discourage us, however; instead it can remind us that we are all works in progress, that God is working faithfully in our lives to complete the work that He started. This is part of what it means to live in the human economy, traveling through life together and connecting to God and people in a profoundly human way. This human way involves embracing the fullness of who we are—the good and the bad parts, the beauty and the brokenness—and remembering that to be human means to be imperfect and flawed, while simultaneously being God's unimaginable masterpiece and treasure.

When Bono, the social activist and lead singer of the band U2, was asked about how he viewed himself, he said, "I do see the good in people, but I also see the bad—I see it in myself. I know what I'm capable of, good and bad. It's very important that we make that clear. Just because I often find a way around the darkness doesn't mean that I don't know it's there."[2] Human beings have both good and bad in them, and the journey of transformation is moving toward more good and less bad. Maybe this is a more extensive journey for us to embrace this reality deeper, but at a foundational level we must understand the profound implications this has for our leadership and relationships. This journey involves beginning to fully embrace ourselves as God does, in our beauty and our brokenness, in our goodness and our deficiencies, in our light and our darkness.

The less accurately we see ourselves, the easier it is to forget our humanity, and even lose sight of who we are in God's eyes. No matter how many flaws, deficits, or dysfunctions we have, we can be reminded that God's love for us never changes. His perspective of every human being is always filled with the fullness of His love, and that's what we hold in dynamic tension of being both humbly honest about our flaws and at the same time confident in who we've been created to be. This is the journey toward true and authentic self-discovery.

An Unexamined Life

The *Harvard Business Review* published an article titled "Discovering Your Authentic Leadership." In it are the results of the largest in-depth study ever undertaken on how authentic leadership fuels effectiveness and success. The article describes a critical component that every great leader needs in his or her journey toward authentic leadership. In one study, when seventy-five members of the Stanford Graduate School of Business Advisory Council were asked to recommend the most important capability for leaders to develop, their answer was nearly unanimous: self-awareness.[3] In this article we discover the truth that if we want to gain an accurate view of ourselves, we must consistently invest in *our internal growth potential*, not just in our external success. This article reveals that an unexamined life is an ineffective life.

> If we want to gain an accurate view of ourselves, we must consistently invest in *our internal growth potential*, not just in our external success.

When we find the courage to look inside without allowing the filters of self-protection and self-preservation to blind us, it opens up a vista to personal growth that we never thought possible. We'll begin to see how we sometimes short-circuit our relationships, and how we use our power and influence inappropriately. As our self-awareness goes up, our relational intelligence goes up. This is why self-awareness is critical to learning this new way of being smart.

Seeing with New Eyes

I was practically blind when I was a teenager, and didn't even know it. When my mom took me to the eye doctor for the first time, the optometrist asked me what I did for fun, and I told him I played baseball. With a perplexed look on his face, he asked, "How exactly do you see the ball?"

My mom immediately interjected with concern: "What do you mean?"

The doctor said, "Your son can't see the ball until it's six inches from his face."

I had a hard time absorbing what he had just said because this was a shocking discovery for me. I always thought that everyone else saw what I saw. It never crossed my mind that I had poor eyesight. As you can imagine, my immediate solution was to get prescription lenses that would help me see more clearly, and what followed changed my baseball future.

After I got contact lenses during the middle of my high school baseball season, my batting average skyrocketed. At first, my coaches and teammates thought that luck was on my side. But when it turned into weeks of continued improvement, they were curious to know the real reason behind my new success. I had begun the season as a mediocre hitter but soon maintained the highest batting average on the team. In one season, my batting average climbed more than a hundred points, and my improved ability to see catapulted my baseball career into another dimension. In fact, a few years later I went on to receive a Division One baseball scholarship to the University of South Carolina (and by the way, that's the *real* USC, founded long before the University of Southern California).

My growing success in baseball traced back to identifying my greatest limitation: my inability to see clearly. After the doctor helped me make the necessary adjustments to improve my vision, the results that followed were extraordinary. I was opened up to a whole new world of seeing what I never saw before. I could see more clearly what I was swinging at, and I hit the ball with more force, precision, and impact.

Prescribing a New Lens

The path toward increasing our greatest leadership impact begins with honestly acknowledging our inability to see ourselves clearly. As we acknowledge our blind spots and identify our limitations, we can make adjustments that allow us to improve our vision, and we can begin to develop a new level of ability that strengthens our leadership force, precision, and impact. We may never be able to eliminate all our blind spots, but the more we can acknowledge them the more we deny their power over us. Other people will start to wonder about the secret to our new success, and our new success will be seen in how we relate to people. They will see healthier, deeper, and more connected relationships. They will see trust and credibility emerge quickly, and they'll watch as it creates exponential leadership influence. They'll see not just an expanding quantity of relationships, but a growing quality in them.

Let's say your blind spot is that people on your teams see you as intimidating and unapproachable, but you don't see yourself that way. This may result in others not offering their opinions or suggestions in team meetings because you make them feel uncomfortable. Or it may result in a surface-level relationship because people don't feel safe with you, and therefore they remain relationally distant to protect themselves. But if you begin to recognize this reality in your relationships, you can be more intentional about identifying how you interact with people and how you might come across as intimidating or relationally unsafe. In the effort to overcome your tendency to be perceived as intimidating, you can be more intentional about inviting people to give their suggestions, and you can affirm them when they do offer their opinion in front of you.

Lack of awareness can manifest in many ways. Maybe you always contradict yourself and don't realize it, and it results in having less credibility with those around you. Maybe people don't feel as valued by you as you think they do, and instead they feel used but you don't even know it. Or maybe you don't collaborate with the people on your teams as well as you think you do and your team members conclude it's a one-man show— and you don't even realize it. Whatever your blind spots are, remember that we all have them, and the journey is to recognize them as clearly as possible to help us overcome their negative effects in our relational world and leadership endeavors.

Curing the Condition

We've discussed why self-awareness is so critical to RI and identified the importance of clarity and awareness in the growth process. Now, let's identify three life habits that can help increase your self-awareness and RI. These are habits, which means they're not something you do once; they are intended to become a new way of living that will lead to increased RI over time. This will help us cure the condition of MSS that we all have.

Habit One: Learn to Access the Perceptions of Those Around You

Have you ever seen a photograph of yourself and thought, "That doesn't look anything like me?" Maybe it wasn't the best angle. Maybe it wasn't your most attractive moment. Maybe you even felt like a celebrity who had a distorted portrait that was published in *People* magazine. But when you see a photograph of yourself that "doesn't look anything like you," unfortunately this is indeed what you looked like from that vantage point, on that day. You just don't always get to see yourself from the angle that others see you from, or that you want them to see you from. It might be hard to admit it, but photographs don't lie (except in *People* magazine).

> It might be hard to admit it, but photographs don't lie. You just don't always get to see yourself from the angle that others see you from, or that you want them to see you from.

This same dynamic is revealed in leadership. There is a discrepancy between leaders' view of themselves and others' view of them. The truth is, the people around us are often much more discerning than what we give them credit for. Because it is impossible to see ourselves accurately from every vantage point, we need to learn how to access the perceptions of those around us. They can be our greatest gift in self-discovery, but it takes intention and courage to identify those perceptions. Perhaps we fear knowing what they are, or maybe we underestimate their importance. As leaders we need mirrors in the form of the people in our lives who can help us see from a variety of angles and allow us to see ourselves accurately.

A friend of mine was caught off guard recently, when someone he highly respected told him, "In some ways, you are better than you think you are, but in other ways, you are not as good as you think you are." Think about that for a moment. On the one hand, this person, whom my friend respects, is addressing his overinflated view of himself. On the other hand, he's pointing out that he is falling short of his potential (and he knows it). Sometimes we see ourselves better than we are and remain out of touch with our deficits. Other times, we feel like an inadequate failure because we're not living up to who we know we can be. No matter which side we're standing on, we're often afraid to hear the truth about ourselves. Sometimes the fear of being exposed stops us from the pursuit of honesty from those around us. When I was a kid, my favorite cartoon show was *G.I. Joe*. Every day after school, I raced home to watch it because I was enthralled with the guns that shot red and blue light beams. My favorite combat soldiers were Snake Eyes and Flint, and I especially loved when they all yelled in concert, "Yoooo, Joe!!" As I got older, my friends stopped watching cartoons like *G.I. Joe* and moved on (to more mature after-school shows such as *Saved by the Bell*). But I wasn't quite ready to let go, so I'd strategically not invite my friends over after school anymore because I didn't want them to know that I still watched it. I hid this secret life for a long time, and then I just decided to come out of the closet. Even today, I secretly want to collect the newest *G.I. Joe* figures (which I've discovered you can still find at Toys "R" Us).

As adults, we often face similar dynamics of hiding things from others that we don't want them to see. In an effort to maintain a better image of ourselves, we fuel our own naïve belief that people don't see our flaws, insecurities, limitations, and even weaknesses. We subtly convince ourselves that every thought they have about us is positive. Or maybe we think they are not scrutinizing our motives simply because we haven't scrutinized ourselves. Truth is, there are many people who can see us with uncanny precision, especially if we are in a leadership position, because they watch more closely than we think. They see how our flaws affect our relationships, and they often see it better than we do. People can even sense whether we're healthy or unhealthy by recognizing the invisible motives that drive our behavior. They can often tell when we're being manipulative, and they can usually sense when we're using people for our own selfish agenda. They can discern when we're genuine and when we truly want the best for people. If our outcomes are successful, they even know when we're shortcutting the appropriate process or when we're doing everything with integrity. People watch how all this affects our interactions, and ultimately our capacity to lead and influence them.

Knowing that some may see us more clearly than we see ourselves, why wouldn't we invite them to share their perceptions to help us navigate our complex inner world? Sure, it's dangerous, a little scary, and vulnerable to invite them in. And though you certainly don't need to invite anybody and everybody into that intimate space, those who can be trusted may have more insight to offer than you've ever known. People don't always offer their opinions in a healthy and constructive way, so you must ask. If you don't ask for it, you may never get it. What often helps is to ask someone to think about it for a few days, and then you can initiate getting together with them after they've had time to think about it. This usually helps them think through the best way to say it to you so that you'll receive it, understand it, and be better off for it.

These insights and vantage points of others can contribute profoundly to improving your RI and ultimately expanding your influence with others. We may be tempted to ignore the implications of other people's perceptions because we falsely believe that our position, or level of status, automatically ensures trust and respect. But instead of ignoring people's perceptions or pretending we don't have flaws, we ought to find wise and appropriate ways to benefit from them. Remember, it begins by simply asking.

Relationships of Honesty

Seeking to gain a view of ourselves that is more accurate doesn't mean that everyone else's view is always correct, nor does it mean that our view is always incorrect. But it does mean that others play an important role when it comes to increasing self-awareness. To become more relationally intelligent, we must learn to foster and receive feedback from people who can extract insight from some of our best moments, as well as from some of our worst. This sparks new dimensions of self-discovery.

A few years ago, I had a defining moment in my life that brought both pain and truth. What led me to this moment started back in college when I had a life-changing encounter with Jesus. In the weeks that followed, friends of mine recognized the changes happening in me, and they began asking me for spiritual guidance. I was young, so I'm not sure how much my advice helped. In those weeks, however, my passion was ignited to guide people in their spiritual curiosity and introduce them to what it meant to have a relationship with God. This passion drove me to help people in their spiritual journey. At one point, I decided to live out this passion as a church planter, which I believed was the optimal way for me to have an impact.

For the next few years, I trained to become a church planter. I paid thousands of dollars and spent hundreds of hours in study,

internships, personal development, and mentoring relationships. I pursued planting a church every step of the way. I was
100 percent invested in this pursuit.

One night I had dinner with a mentor whom I admired. He
knew me well, and as we discussed my future I asked for advice
on my church planting endeavors. I had always given a lot of
weight to his insight about me. After I told him my thoughts,
plans, and strategy, he looked across the table with a spirit of
love and honesty, and by his demeanor I knew he was going to
say something I didn't expect. What he told me was difficult for
me to hear, as he said, "Steve, I don't think you'd be the best
church planter."

Ouch.

I was shocked, offended, disappointed, and hurt. In that
moment, I was hoping for affirmation, encouragement, and
support, but instead I received his gut-level honesty. All those
years, all that money, all that investment—for him to tell me
that? Who knew that one simple statement could create such
chaos and disappointment within me?

But in the coming weeks, as I thought about what he had said
and talked with others who knew me, I realized he was more right
that I wanted to admit. It certainly wasn't an easy process for me,
but this defining moment reminded me of the importance of having people in my life who are willing to tell me the unfiltered
truth about what they see in me. It doesn't mean they're always
right, but these types of relationships are what every leader needs
to become relationally intelligent. To engage in honest relationships like this helps us improve our RI. If I had not invited this
mentor to speak honestly with me, I might have continued down
a path that would not have been my most optimal route. He
helped me see what I couldn't see, and it's helped me further my
leadership potential in ways I would never have imagined.

Of course, we must be wise in whom we invite into that
intimate relational space to speak honestly into our lives and
address what we might not see clearly. I remember one day when
I left the stage after speaking, and someone walked backstage to

find me. She held up a full page of written feedback about things she said she had to tell me so that I could be a better speaker. I said firmly but graciously, "Thanks for offering your feedback, but I have other people who know me well whom I've already asked for input." It was a thanks-but-no-thanks moment as I tried to handle her lack of relational intelligence in the most gracious but firm way possible.

Certainly, there will be people who attempt to enter whom we haven't invited to have a voice in our lives, but there are appropriate ways to create boundaries for them. In an effort to improve our approach, here are a few brief guidelines on whom to invite into that space. These are ideal, and of course we may not necessarily find all of these facets in one person, but they can serve to guide us.

Is willing to be honest, but speaks the truth in love
Recognizes our potential and believes the best in us
Embodies gentle strength
Has a humble desire to be helpful and serve us well
Is seen as wise and insightful
Knows us well and has the ability to be specific in feedback
Is trustworthy

Don't forget to be this kind of person yourself.

In choosing whom we bring into personal and honest conversation, we need to look for people who are willing to be honest enough with us to say difficult things that might be hard to hear. Along the way, of course, we should not limit our openness only to people who simply make us feel better about ourselves. In fact, there should definitely be some people who practically make us nervous about what they might say because they are willing to be so completely honest. Many times, if the conversation becomes painful, it often means they're closing in on a persistent blind spot. These kinds of relationships enlighten us; we begin to see ourselves with new eyes and, as a result, increase our relational intelligence.

A Word of Caution: Knowing the Truth About Yourself

> In seeking people to help you identify your blind spots, don't
> limit yourself to those who always agree with you. People who
> are yes-men say things that make us feel good, which everyone
> seems to enjoy. But that's not going to help us much in unveiling
> our blind spots. Many of us create circles of friends who are yes-
> men because we are afraid of the truth. Our ego is so fragile that
> we'd rather avoid the pain that comes with honesty and truth. But
> if we want honest feedback and input about our relationships,
> leadership, and even character, then it will demand courage to
> overcome these unseen yet powerful fears, and invite others into
> our vulnerable relational space.

Finding honest relationships doesn't necessarily need to be a formal process. It's more about a lifestyle of inviting people into our relational space where we let them openly speak into our lives. This is about inviting people to analyze, critique, and evaluate us—hopefully in the spirit of love. It's about freeing people to make suggestions that help us grow in self-awareness, and ultimately in RI. Then of course we must decide what to do with their input and feedback.

Voices of Wisdom

There's a proverb that says, "Wisdom shouts from the rooftops." This is absolutely true, but it's amazing how we continuously find ways to ignore it. Wisdom is available to us in many forms and from many places. One of the primary places to find it is in the people around us, whom we trust and respect. But it is our responsibility to turn our attention to accessing that wisdom from the voices of people we trust and respect. We are responsible for inviting their honesty, and if we do we'll be tapping into an unlimited resource to help us on our journey toward self-discovery. When we as leaders value honest relationships as a way of life, it has a ripple effect on how it affects others.

Habit Two: Learn to Activate the Reflective Mind Within You

Another way to cure the Michael Scott Syndrome is through learning to activate the reflective mind within us. By this I mean the consistent habit of gaining insight through replaying situations in our minds. Every one of us has the ability to reflect and learn from it. The best athletes in the world watch films of previous games so they can see and learn from what they did well, and what they did poorly. They often spend hours and hours studying their performance in an effort to become the best they can be because they know that an unexamined life is an ineffective life. Too often we don't pay close enough attention to examining our relational interactions, which as a result causes us to keep making the same mistakes time and time again.

Recently, I was watching Oprah (as I was just passing by the TV, of course) interviewing a family from a reality TV program about their everyday life. The show is called *Little People, Big World*. It's an inside look at a family of little people going about their everyday lives. At one point, Oprah turned to the father of the family and asked, "What are the challenges of having your lives so exposed on film for the world to see?" He said, "Actually, it's been less of a challenge and more of a catalyst for growth in my personal development." He went on to describe that he watches every episode after it is filmed. As he watches, he observes the nuances of his interactions with his family. He sees his moods, behaviors, and attitudes, as well as noticing how his values are fleshed out in his everyday relationships.

He recalled one specific example when he was watching an episode. While he was working on his computer, his son walked up and asked him a question. As he watched the replay of this scene, he saw the subtle annoyance he expressed because of the interruption. By his own admission, he realized that this was a missed opportunity with his son. In essence, he had lacked RI in that moment. In the unconscious awareness of his aggravation, he pushed his son away and unknowingly hurt the boy's feelings. From that moment on, he decided he was never again going to make his computer a priority over his son. He described how he never would have seen the impact of his actions, and the subtle posture of his heart toward his son, if he had not seen it on camera afterward. He explained how it made him sad to see how unaware he was of his own interpersonal behavior.

Most of us don't have the luxury of pulling out the films of our reality show so we can work to become better men or women, but we are capable of watching the ins and outs of our daily lives in the context of our mind. Through our thoughts, we can replay the virtual video of our actions, attitudes, and words as they relate to our interactions with others. We can reflect on how we treat and interact with others, how our conversation could have gone better, or how our mood negatively affected a certain scenario.

I try to walk away from every leadership team meeting I lead reflecting on what I could I have done differently. For example, I may ask myself what I could have added to the conversation, or what I should not have said that I now regret. I sometimes wonder what results, outcomes, or goals came from the meeting, and I ponder whether the decisions were the right ones. I ask questions of this kind and ponder the flow of the meeting in my mind, hoping to learn. I know that I don't have control of what other people say or do, but I always try to learn how I could have said or done something better in that meeting. And if I said something that offended someone else, I try to apologize, or at least check in with that person to make sure everything is all right between us. These reflections help me think more thoroughly about relational dynamics and inevitably help me increase my RI.

The Cost of Reflection

If you're wondering why more people don't practice more reflective thinking, I wonder the same thing. I'm not convinced that we don't value reflection, but I do think we tend to avoid the cost that comes with practicing it because the cost involves time, effort, and sometimes even personal pain. As we replay a specific situation, we may realize how and why we failed, and this can be hard to swallow. When our failure to execute produces negative consequences, it bothers us because we realize it could have gone differently. We see how one altered decision could have changed the negative outcome. And when we see these painful mistakes, we also become more sensitive to our regrets. All this is hard to deal with because we realize what we should have done and where we didn't measure up. At the same time, mistakes create a context for transformational learning.

There are other costs of reflection that may involve going back to fix a problem we created or mend a broken relationship. But no matter the cost, developing the discipline of reflection is worth it because it can accelerate our growth in self-awareness, and therefore enhance the quality and depth of our relationships. If you engage this quest to become more self-aware, you'll hurt people less, help people more, and create a distinctly more positive relational culture around you.

> If you engage this quest to become more self-aware, you'll hurt people less, help people more, and create a distinctly more positive relational culture around you.

Habit Three: Write Clarifying Statements

The third habit to develop involves gaining clarity. If we think of our blind spots in vague terms, it's much like telling a doctor that we are in pain without clarifying where the pain is. Not knowing the location of the pain is unhelpful to the doctor because her treatment or prescription is entirely dependent on our ability to describe where the pain is and what it feels like. This is sometimes what we do with our blind spots: we know we have them ("the pain"), but we just don't know where they are; therefore we aren't able to identify the prescription or treatment needed to manage or overcome their negative effects. At best, we may use vague sweeping statements to describe that we have them ("I know I have weaknesses, but everybody does, so what's the big deal?" "I know I have character issues, but I'm trying to improve."). But without becoming more specific, we will stunt our capacity to cultivate healthy relationships.

The first two habits help us look more closely at our blind spots, and as we gain their insights, it can be helpful to practice this third habit by clearly writing down the insights we've gained from others and through reflection. If we want to increase our relational intelligence, we must learn how to identify our blind spots clearly and specifically, while also paying attention to how they affect our leadership and relationships. Naming our specific blind spots can help us know which specific prescription or treatment is needed.

In effort to get us started in this process, here are a few examples of some common blind spots:

- I struggle with becoming easily envious of others' accomplishments, so I get discouraged about my ability to succeed when certain people in my field—even friends—have success.

- I get easily insecure about my own sense of worth and value, so when not enough attention is on me from my supervisor or coworkers, I feel devalued and internally weak.

- I usually think of myself as wanting to build others up, but in reality I find myself putting others down in effort to deal with my own deficiencies.

- When I make decisions, I often fail to consider the opinions of others on the team, and it often stifles team cohesiveness and ownership.

- I usually think of myself as a good listener, but the truth is I have a reputation of always talking about myself rather than focusing genuinely and unselfishly on others.

- I like to be in a position of control, and it's hard for me to let others lead.

- I often think of myself as warm and personable, but when I take an honest look at myself I tend to come off as aloof and impersonal.

These are common examples of writing clarifying statements that we may resonate with, or at least that might get us thinking about our own blind spots. This will certainly take additional reflection as well as vulnerability and honesty on our part. There are numerous resources that have helped me, and others, identify and process blind spots, so here are a few to help you go further and deeper.

- *The Leadership Challenge* has a 360-degree feedback tool that you can take with those around you to help give you insight in your own self-awareness (more info at www.leadershipchallenge.com).

- The Myers-Briggs Type Indicator is a popular assessment tool to help people identify their personality preferences; it can also help point to blind spots (that is, which things are *not* preferences). There are innumerable Web sites, books, and other materials related to the MBTI.

- The Character Matrix is an assessment to help someone identify strengths and weaknesses of character and become more self-aware of character-related matters in life that may be blind spots. (More info on www.relationalintelligence.info)

- Other tools include the Taylor-Johnson Temperament Analysis (http://www.tjta.com), the DISC Personality Profile (http://www.onlinediscprofile.com), and the Gallup Strengths Finder (http://www.strengthsfinder.com).

What If We Don't?

Without developing a keen sense of self-awareness, how we relate to people may be no more than accidental. If our philosophy becomes "ignorance is bliss," or if we feel that "everyone has weakness so who cares," then the quality of our relationships and influence will certainly suffer. To be sure, we don't always have control over the outcomes of our leadership endeavors or how others choose to relate to us, but we do have control over how we treat people, how we relate to them, and who we become in the process. If we ignore our blind spots and refuse to seek the accurate truth about ourselves, we will overlook critical components of our leadership impact.

True self-awareness guides us more accurately down the path toward becoming who we really long to become in both our leadership and our relationships. We begin to better understand who we truly are and move toward who we really want to become. This inevitably fuels unimaginable influence and a relationally centered approach to our leadership. If we desire to expand our influence, we must push through the muddied waters of self-denial into the clarity that self-awareness brings.

PART
2

The Hidden Power of a Relational Genius

Thousands of geniuses live and die undiscovered—
either by themselves, or by others.

— MARK TWAIN[1]

Who comes to mind when you think of genius? Maybe it's Albert Einstein, a mathematical genius who came up with a little thing called $E = mc^2$ (not to mention the Theory of Relativity). Or maybe Howard Hughes pops up because, although some consider him a madman, he was a creative genius through his groundbreaking work in both aviation and film. In the world of music, maybe you think of Mozart or Beethoven, both of whom had the capacity to hold up to six or seven melodies in their mind at the same time, while simultaneously understanding how those melodies interacted with each other. Then there are some modern-day geniuses. I can't help but think about both of the twentysomething creators of YouTube. In less than twenty-four months, they figured out how to create, launch, and sell their Web site to Google for $1.65 billion. Who knew that home videos could generate that kind of money? Now, that's genius!

There's something about a genius in any field that inspires people. Maybe it's because they explore unknown territory, or because they invent things we've never thought of before, or because they break new ground by doing what the rest of us think is impossible. Or maybe we're simply inspired by how they use their extraordinary talents to make the world a better place. Whatever the reasons, there's no doubt it would be a tragedy if they never took time to use and develop their genius. Just think about it: wouldn't it be a terrible waste if the people we know to be geniuses never actualized their extraordinary abilities?

I'm convinced that every human being has an underdeveloped relational genius within. Every one of us has the capacity to actualize his or her own genius. I believe this power exists within you, and that one of your great challenges involves focusing your time, energy, and intentionality on identifying, developing, and unleashing the hidden power of your own relational genius. Like geniuses in other arenas, this can become your arena to achieve uncharted

> Every human being has an underdeveloped relational genius within.

brilliance and make the world a better place, but it's up to you whether you'll seize this reality in your life, leadership, and relationships.

The path to becoming a relational genius is not impeded by a specific personality type or temperament, or by having certain life experiences, and it's not dependent on your background or history. Nor is it just for people who are extremely extroverted, who have natural charisma, or who easily win over others. And it's not even limited by specific God-given talents we do or do not have. Of course there are different facets to developing our relational genius that come easier to some people than others, but anybody who is willing to step up to the challenge can embody this new way of being smart. What I am declaring here is what Albert Einstein once profoundly declared of our potential as human beings: "There's a genius in all of us."

What Does a Relational Genius Look Like?

Though we may have not fully realized it, I anticipate that all of us have encountered a relational genius. It's almost impossible to ignore the brilliance of how they engage interpersonally with others. Relational geniuses have mastered the art of doing relationships well, and they embody an exceptional capacity to cultivate healthy and dynamic relationships. How they interact with others stands out because they know how to authentically connect with diverse people in meaningful and positively productive ways. It's hard not to be pulled into a conversation with them, or be compelled to listen to what they have to say. They carry positive social energy, they're remarkably likeable and magnetic, they're genuinely interested *in* people, and they're curiously interesting *to* people. They move conversations forward with intention and understand the power of investing in people wisely and strategically. As we discover what a relational genius looks and acts like, we'll begin to realize what differentiates them from others. It is the way they've learned to apply relational intelligence to everyday life, leadership, and relationships.

But maybe you wonder about a relational genius because you want to become one. Maybe you wonder what the defining characteristics are of "a genius of relationships." And maybe the question swirling around in that brilliant mind of yours is, How might someone go about developing and maximizing those relational genius qualities, striving to gain relational influence, cultivate relational health, and enhance the quality of every relationship in life?

Glad you asked.

There are six defining roles I've observed that can guide you toward actualizing the hidden power of your relational genius— that one that exists within. This is not an exhaustive list of roles, but ones that are essential to the quest to increase your relational intelligence and develop a new kind of genius. Some traits may not be what you expect, but they all have a profound impact on your leadership effectiveness and your ongoing interpersonal world. In the next six chapters, we'll discuss how you can discover the hidden power of your relational genius.

Six Defining Roles of a Relational Genius

1. The Story Collector
2. The Energy Carrier
3. The Compelling Relator
4. The Conversational Futurist
5. The Likeable Hero
6. The Disproportionate Investor

The Story Collector

To be a person is to have a story to tell.

—*Isak Dinesen*[1]

One sign of success in a given relationship is when a person feels known. People feel most known when the story their life is telling gets heard and understood. The path to helping a person feel known involves learning to be a *story collector*—that is, someone who draws out the story of people's lives with genuine interest. When someone is relationally intelligent, he or she cultivates relationships where people are able to share the most interesting facets of their life story. This is not necessarily easy to do, but simple in concept. To do it, there's one primal requirement: *be interested in people*.

The Apostle Paul once declared, "Do nothing out of selfish ambition or vain conceit; but in humility consider others better than yourselves. Each of you should look not only to your own interests but also to the interests of others."[2]

People feel known when we strongly identify with a distinct part of who they are, or when we recognize a unique facet of their humanness. People feel understood when we help them express, or step into, more of who they are as a human being. To increase our RI, we must learn how to become more interested in others by exploring the story their lives are telling. We can learn how to identify aspects of who they are that are different from anyone else. This doesn't mean we make a person feel fully known in a moment when one part of her story is told, because knowing someone fully takes a lifetime to do. However, becoming relationally intelligent does involve getting better at making people feel known in a short window of time through listening and connecting to their story. Although we cannot see and discover every facet of a human being in a passing moment, we can recognize, and strongly identify with, a part of his essence that is unique to him. When it comes to being interested in people, the goal is not to be interested in every detail of their lives, but rather to discover what is interesting about them and draw it out.

> When it comes to being interested in people, the goal is not to be interested in every detail of their lives, but rather to discover what is interesting about them and draw it out.

No matter where your interaction falls on the spectrum (which ranges from meeting someone new in a social context, to working with a team of volunteers, to engaging in a mentoring relationship, to trying to strengthen a friendship, or to our daily interactions at work), being interested in people is a critical component of RI that advances relationships. Human beings long for their story to be known, and most of us live our lives without consistently experiencing this as a pervasive and deeper reality in our personal world.

The best-selling author Patrick Lencioni identifies this reality as it plays out in the workplace. Discussing the importance of feeling known at work, he says, "The first sign of a miserable job is anonymity, which is the feeling that employees get when they realize that their manager has little interest in them as a human being, and that they know little about their lives, their aspirations, and their interests."[3] Essentially, he's saying that people remain miserable in their work environment when they don't feel known or understood by their boss. The truth is, not only do people feel this at work but it is a pervasive reality in all of life, relationships, and leadership. We will be at a standstill in our leadership endeavors, and probably be regressing, if we don't activate our relational skills to discover what's most interesting about others through how we lead and interact with them.

Dimensions Reveal Value

Our showing interest in something begins with recognizing its value. When relational geniuses interact with people, they seek to find the distinct value of a human being. In a similar way, a diamond is multifaceted, and although in a brief moment we're not able to grasp hold of its value in its entirety, we are able to identify certain facets. If we hold up a diamond in the sunlight and twist it around to observe its multidimensional nature, we're able to see certain qualities that make it uncommon and therefore valuable. In the same way, relational geniuses can be the light that reveals the internal, and sometimes unseen, beauty of another human being. They know how to identify specific facets of a person by peering into the prism of her core and finding what makes her shine.

In an effort to help the average guy find the right diamond for the woman he loves (which can be much easier than finding the right woman *to* love), expert diamontologists developed a simple way to assess the value of a diamond. They organized it around four categories referred to as "the four C's of diamonds" (cut, color, clarity, and weight in carats). This is a basic way for people to understand the value of something as complex as a diamond, especially for us guys who are usually clueless when it comes to jewelry.

All of us generically know that diamonds are valuable, meaning we understand their worth in a general way. Similarly, we generically know that human beings are valuable, but we don't always recognize how each individual person carries his own worth unique to him. The four C's of diamonds help us take our generic knowledge to a more intricate understanding of what makes a specific diamond valuable in itself. These C's reveal ways to recognize the diamond's value in certain dimensions. As human beings, we also can learn how to better identify the value in every person whose path we cross and discover what makes her distinctly valuable in her own way. One way to do this is by developing our own version of the four C's.

Secrets of the Story Collector

The secret behind great story collectors is that they know the right things to look for. Just as the four C's give us four categories to help us determine the value of a diamond, story collectors begin with three categories or facets that help them discover what distinguishes an individual person from the masses. Through this framework, they're able to see different dimensions of a person more clearly and with more depth. This helps them draw out the story people's lives are telling. When we hear any story, we know it is best when it is told in an interesting way, which means that the path toward becoming a story collector involves improving our ability to draw out other people's story in a more interesting way.

Every one of us can become a great story collector, and the journey begins by identifying the three facets (categories) to use that can guide our pursuit. Story collectors focus on drawing out the *dreams, life history, and personhood* of the people in their lives. To increase our relational intelligence, we must begin to see ourselves as story collectors and allow these three facets to serve as our framework in identifying and drawing out what's most interesting about a person's story. This will result in making others feel known, and at the same time will open our eyes to the most interesting dimensions of their humanity. It is possible to increase our capacity to be interested in others by cultivating our ability to draw out the most interesting facets of another human being.

The Art of Good Question Asking

If we want to learn how to discover the unique facets of a person's dreams, life history, and personhood, the primary skill to develop is the art of good question asking. If we want to become great story collectors, we must become great question askers.

> If we want to become great story collectors, we must become great question askers.

Story collectors know how to use the power of questions to steer conversation to a more interesting place and draw out distinct facets of people's story.

Although most people lean on generic question asking for conversation starters, questions of this kind tend to evoke predictable, safe responses, ones that are simplistic in nature. Although these questions are usually asked with sincerity, they are still elementary and don't help us discover the deeper dimensions of who a person is or what is truly interesting about them.

Some generic questions that are frequently asked in conversation are "Where are you from?" "What do you do for work?" "What school did you go to?" Unfortunately, people tend to answer these types of questions with very little thought, which usually makes their answers less than compelling. Most generic question asking doesn't drive conversation to a deeper, more intriguing place, and they don't unveil the layered nuances of what distinguishes one person from the rest. Becoming interested in people is not about discovering facts or information about them but exploring what drives their lives, what makes them different from you and me, and what has shaped who they've become.

In an effort to move away from generic question asking and uncover deeper dimensions of people's story, here are some don'ts and dos that can help you become a better story collector.

Don'ts and Dos of Story Collectors

1. Don't start a conversation by talking about yourself.
   Instead, ask people about their story and interests—and listen genuinely.
2. Don't allow your conversation to stay at a surface level or remain generic in nature.
   Instead, strive to move people past the surface into deeper dialogue through thoughtful questions.
3. Don't ask simplistic questions that result in short or yes-no answers.
   Instead, ask open-ended questions that draw out the uniqueness of people's story.

If we want to learn how to uncover other people's dreams, life history, and personhood, we must begin developing the specific relational skill set of good question asking. To do this, let's look at these three facets of human uniqueness that can help us draw out people's most interesting self.

Facet One: Dreams

Knowing the dreams that reside in the heart of human beings is one of the most primal elements in understanding their essence and discovering their story. By a dream I mean the innate longing a person feels to accomplish something in this life. It may show itself in how a person desires to use a specific gift or talent to serve humanity in some way, or it may be revealed in how someone wants to use a passion to create a better world. Dreams are created as a result of people wanting their lives to count, to leave their mark in history. Dreams fuel our imagination;

they are what give us hope and meaning, and they can be a reflection of a person's destined path in this life. Dreams are what get us up in the morning, and what motivate us to do life well, and what compel us to strive for something better. When we peer into the prism of people's dreams, we can see their souls shine through. What could be more interesting about a person than seeing this window into their soul, namely, their dreams?

> When we peer into the prism of people's dreams, we can see their souls shine through.

There are many ways to discover people's dreams besides just asking, "What do you dream about?" These aspirations are cloaked in many things, and there are many ways to identify what they are by exploring how they're externalized in a person's life. This may include paying closer attention to their career ambitions, what they're passionate about, what risks they've stepped into to make some of their dreams happen, or what courageous decisions they've made in order to propel them toward their greatest ambitions.

I remember the first time I met Jason at Starbucks. I was sipping on my grande nonfat latte, extra hot, with extra foam, which came alongside my ongoing addiction to the Starbucks Cinnamon Swirl Coffee Cake. Meanwhile, Jason slurped down his Naked Orange Juice and indulged in his own apple fritter addiction. Shortly into our conversation, I was immediately impressed with him because what takes most people several con-versations took him only one. In just a few brief moments, he identified certain aspects of my dreams and began to draw them out. I was surprised how interested in me he was. I noticed his intentionality in steering our conversation past the surface into exploring deeper dimensions of who I was. He quickly moved our dialogue past the common, where most conversations with new people stay, and started a conversation that revolved around my longings to effect change in the world. He did this through the art of question asking, and he did it in stages.

He initially began the conversation by asking about the steps I had taken to pursue my aspirations. At one point, he found out that I worked with a nonprofit organization that he admired. When he saw that it was such a defining chapter of my life, and because it was also intriguing to him, he capitalized on this moment of discovery. Then he used it to launch into a series of open-ended and thought-provoking questions: "What difficult choices and sacrifices did you make in order to enter into this calling?" "How did this influence the way your future took shape?" "What were your greatest successes and failures along the way?" "Did you ever doubt your abilities at times to follow this dream through, and how did you thrive or survive in those moments?" "How did pursuing your dreams lead you to this point in time in which my path and yours intersected?" It's almost as if Jason, through his questions, took me through a series of tunnels, one leading deeper into the next. I gradually found myself sharing some of my greatest joys and most profound struggles connected to my dreams. Jason guided this all with intention and direction.

As he investigated this facet of my life, his interest in me expanded. I shared sacred parts of my story, and it authenticated the experience I had with him that day, because in the process of his being interested in me he made me feel known and understood. This opened the door for a genuine friendship to begin, which has not only lasted years but has been one of mutual partnering in achieving one another's dreams. In fact, we still make occasional trips to Starbucks, as we indulge in our addictions as well as share our dreams with one another.

In essence, he drew out dreams that were distinct to my story, and through our dialogue he invited me to share things that were of core importance to me. I felt more understood by him in that short but meaningful encounter than I ever had in some of my long-lasting friendships. Jason's genuine interest in me drove his relational genius, and he simultaneously steered our interaction toward something about me that also interested him.

QUESTIONS TO ASK ABOUT DREAMS

In an effort to draw out the distinct aspirations of others, here are three pairs of examples to contrast how you could improve your question asking and increase your RI.

EXAMPLE 1
Generic: "Do you like your job?" A response might be, "Yes, I love it." or "No, I hate it."

Open ended: If you ask someone, "How's work going lately?" and if she seems discontented, you could ask a follow-up question, such as, "If you could do anything, what would it be?" or "Have you thought about doing something else for work, and if so, how have you pursued doing that?"

EXAMPLE 2
Generic: "What have you been doing lately?" A response might be, "I've been training for a marathon."

Open ended: "What motivates you to put such extraordinary effort into training for a marathon?" or "What gives you the drive to keep training?"

EXAMPLE 3
Generic: "What do you do for work?" A response might be, "I'm a consultant."

Open ended: "What dreams and passions led you to take your job, and what's most fulfilling about it?"

Open ended questions almost always evoke more interesting responses.

As a result of his combining the value of being interested in me with what's intriguing to him, there was a more dynamic and energized component to our interactions. In other words, we both gained something valuable from our time together because the conversation engaged both people's interest level.

Developing our ability to be interested in people requires our ability to draw out their most interesting dimensions.

Jason is an example to me, more than ever, of what it looks like to be interested in others in a way that grows the quality and success of relationships. Not only does he still do this today but he's better at it than ever because he's been actively developing this relational skill set while striving to live out this value for years. He's one of the best people I know at moving encounters with people through the stages of making people feel known. And he does it better, and gets there faster, than anyone else I know. In this instance, he showed his interest in my story through exploring the human prism of dreams.

Facet Two: Life History

Making people feel known not only comes through understanding their dreams but also involves exploring the story of their past. Once you understand certain aspects of a person's life history, it's as if you're opening up a book that is their life and reading through the chapters of what they've been through. In a sense, everyone's life is a walking novel waiting to be read with anticipation. In the process, we begin to discover the experiences that reveal their unfolding plot and the characters in their story. Who are the heroes and villains? Where was their rescue, and where was their abandonment? Where was their great love and sacrifice, and where was their neglect and mistreatment? How did their greatest successes and greatest failures shape their quest in this life?

Taking time to listen to what occurred in the space of people's lives can be a powerful medium for making people feel known, whether it's someone we've been entrusted to lead, a person who sits next to us at work, or someone we call a friend, despite having never inquired about their past.

> Everyone's life is a walking novel waiting to be read with anticipation.

People's life history is the context where their lives are formed and transformed. There are numerous ways to approach the person we're interacting with, but almost everyone wants the most critical elements of a life story to be heard, at least to some degree. After all, those are aspects of people's lives that helped define their identity and shape the trajectory of their life. However, the weight of our responsibility is not to draw out every detail of people's past, but rather to *identify the most defining moments in their own story.*

One way I zero in on getting to know people's life history is through the context of team development. In an effort to find what is distinct about people on teams I oversee, I often lead retreats because they offer a context for people to creatively and unconventionally share their life story. One way I facilitate this is by asking all the team members to find a scene from a film that captures a core element of their story that has shaped who they are individually. Then, after they show their scene, they explain why it mirrors their life story. At our last retreat, the films ranged from *The Shawshank Redemption* to *Pride and Prejudice*, *Karate Kid*, and even *Nacho Libre*. Before you think it sounds pathetic to have your life reflected in *Nacho Libre*, let me say Johan actually used the film to tell his life journey in a humorous and inventive way, and in a manner that revealed his clever personality and enhanced how we got to know him.

Through this experience, team members are freed to express their story in an original way. This draws out what is unique to their human experience rather than simply presenting information, which can often cause boredom not only for the listener but also for themselves. It can be light-hearted and funny, as in using *Nacho Libre*, or it can be more serious as in using *Shawshank Redemption* or *Good Will Hunting*. Our group was captivated and moved as one person shared a clip from the film *Alive*, about a team of rugby players who survived a plane crash. You may wonder how someone who had never played rugby or been in a plane crash could relate to this film, but as she shared her story it became more evident how the undercurrent of the plot was truer to her experience than one might think at first glance.

There is a scene toward the end of the movie where two of the survivors, after losing most of the men on their team to starvation and freezing temperatures, decided to risk their lives and venture into the cold and endless mountains to find rescue on the other side. In a powerful moment, the two men struggle to climb to the top of a mountain after days of exhausting travel, hoping that at the top they will find their rescue. But as they clear the top, instead of green pastures and warmth they find a view of endless snow-covered mountaintops, which crushes their hope.

One of the men, discouraged and despondent, collapses to the ground and is ready to give up. The other man, played by Ethan Hawke, has a totally different perspective. His gaze stretches across the vast mountains in front of him, and in this moment, he unexpectedly declares that God is with them, pulling them through the past seventy days of climbing and surviving. Instead of seeing the vast obstacles in front of him, he saw the glorious creation of a higher power. Then his friend responded to him by saying, Don't you get it? It ends here. We're all going to die. As Ethan Hawke's character stood with an aura of courage and determination, he acknowledges that death could in fact be the end result for them. However, with a resilient drive to continue on, he declares that if they're going to die, then why not die walking.

Maybe you've seen *Alive*, but for me that scene wasn't as meaningful until the moment on the retreat when this girl shared how her past was filled with what to her seemed insurmountable obstacles: family brokenness, extreme social challenges, immense poverty. She described her journey of loneliness and hopelessness as a kid, not knowing at many points if she'd survive. Then she shared what seemed to be the climax of her story. She described how her first true encounter with God helped her see with a new pair of eyes. She was able to see that the mountains in her life were no longer obstacles but opportunities. If she could walk through what she was facing with courage and determination, she would come out on the other side to a greater life and find that she could overcome her greatest fears. She decided not to give up; if she were going to lose everything, she would lose while fighting with everything she had.

Our whole group was able to see something special in that moment because she allowed us to flip through the chapters of her life. We saw not only the heartache and struggle but also the joy and victory. *We saw how she lived out her greatest role in her own story*, as she survived her past and overcame great challenges. We were given a window into how she found it within herself to fight through it all, and not only survive, but thrive. This changed how we all related to her, and it made her a much more interesting person to us. Instead of sharing a mere time line of her life, she compellingly pulled us into her narrative by giving us a window into her journey.

Wide Open Spaces in the Heart

After retreats of that kind, people always feel extremely known by the rest of the group. It inevitably accelerates group chemistry and helps everyone on the team become more interested in one another. It highlights the distinguishing aspects of people's history that most likely would not have been discovered quite so fast, or in quite the same way. In these moments of knowing, it's not that people get to know everything about one another,

> Story collectors seek to discover scenes from people's lives that are distinguishing components of their story.

but they do discover some of the most fundamentally important things. Certainly, we can't always have people show scenes from a movie to find what's most distinct about them; nor do moments like these require a retreat for this dynamic to happen. Everyone's life is filled with scene after scene telling their story. Story collectors seek to discover scenes from people's lives that are distinguishing components of their story. They ask questions that become like a magnifying glass to help them see those interesting facets of people's past that they couldn't otherwise see.

Something transcendent happens when a person allows you to read through the chapters and view the scenes of his or her life. Most people want to invite us into their unfolding plot because by sharing this moment with them we also become part of their story. All this creates a healthy and dynamic engagement with the people involved on both sides of a relationship. As we discover the unique facets of a person's life history, our interest simultaneously grows, and the person actually becomes more interesting to us.

As we travel together through life, the person who may have been little more than a stranger just a moment earlier is now someone our heart is drawn to. And a certain bond is formed. As a result, we grow more engaged, and it's not just because the information that was shared makes the relationship more interesting but because we have created a wide-open space in our hearts for the other person.

Both Sides of Interesting

Being interested in people is about zeroing in on the most meaningful and defining chapters and scenes of their lives. The goal here isn't to force a conversation to go somewhere the other person doesn't want it to go, but to navigate our relationships in a way that draws out something distinctly unique about another person's life history so he or she feels understood. The more we learn to ask questions with specificity,

> Relational geniuses know how to connect their interest to what's interesting about another person.

QUESTIONS TO ASK ABOUT A LIFE HISTORY

In an effort to draw out the unique life story of others, here are a pair of examples to contrast how you could improve your question asking and increase your RI.

EXAMPLE 1

Generic: "Where are you from? Where did you grow up?"

Open ended: "What type of environment did you grow up in? What were some defining moments in your childhood? How has your past helped shape your present, both positively and negatively?"

EXAMPLE 2

Generic: "How many brothers and sisters do you have?"

Open ended: "What were your family dynamics like when you were growing up, and what was your role in them?"

intention, and direction, the more fully engaged everyone will be in the relationships of our lives because the conversations will revolve around what both people are simultaneously interested in. Relational geniuses know how to connect their interest to what's interesting about another person.

Facet Three: Personhood

When we peer into the prism of other people's lives to find what's most interesting about them, we discover the third facet of story collecting: personhood. This encompasses core identity, personality type, fundamental beliefs, convictions, and values. Personhood is revealed most clearly through the actions and behaviors in someone's outer life, but in actuality it reflects more about the core of their inner life. To understand the essence of personhood, we can compare it to understanding how the cut of a diamond affects its brilliance, which is perhaps the most important of the four C's. Many people confuse the cut with shape, but shape refers to the general outward appearance. (Is it round? Pear? Emerald-shaped?) Cut is a specific reference to a diamond's reflective qualities, which come from the "heart of the diamond." This quality affects the properties and value of the stone because a good cut gives a diamond its brilliance, causing it to explode with light that catches people's eye and adds elegance. (It also elicits "oohs" and "ahhs" from the female population.)

In a similar way, our personhood is what causes us to shine as human beings. This quality isn't determined by outward appearance but is instead our reflective quality coming from within. Just because your inner brilliance may not elicit oohs and ahhs from everyone at first glance, it doesn't mean there's not a beautiful gem that needs to be uncovered. *What's most compelling about someone's personhood is what distinguishes her from the masses, and what makes her feel known at the deepest level.* In fact, it is practically impossible to make a person feel known without exploring some aspect of personhood, mainly identity, core convictions, and personality.

> Our personhood is what causes us to shine as human beings.

"You Really Get Me"

One of the first things Cheri said when we started dating was, "You really *get me*." This is one of the greatest joys in our marriage because it's a unique way of saying, "I feel deeply known by you." This idea of "getting someone" seems so simple, but carries so much weight at the same time. When you understand the personhood of other human beings at a deep level, you get what makes them . . . *them*.

One man I know is an expert at getting people, and he happens to be my father-in-law, Gary. It was a bit scary when I started dating his daughter (but that's a story for another day).

One Sunday afternoon, Gary was in town visiting, and we went to lunch with a group of friends he had never met. This included two of them who were pseudo-dating, meaning everyone else knew they were dating but they weren't ready to make it official yet. After we ordered and sat down, our conversations began. At one point, Gary began chatting with the pseudo-daters, Sarah and Daniel. He asked intentional questions about the nature of their relationship. Before the lunch, my wife and I had clued him in on the ambiguity of their dating status, so it appeared he was trying to move them along a bit.

As Gary asked question after question about them, both individually and as they related to each other, everyone at the table began to listen in. It actually wasn't because Sarah and Daniel had dating drama, although that's often interesting enough for the whole table to listen to. The reason people tuned in was because of how and where Gary was guiding the conversation. He was clearly showing interest in these two in particular. After listening intently, and in combination with observing their behavior, he began offering pertinent insights. (They had been struggling to understand each other, and this was causing a lot of frustration in their relationship.) At one point, Gary offered a dual metaphor of a marathon runner and a sprinter to compare the two of them. He started to compare Sarah to a sprinter who moves hard and fast in life, whether in relationships, in her career, or in other areas of her life. She does it almost to the point of exhausting all her energy up front. She dives into every experience in life headfirst. Although this makes her exciting, and what Gary called "the spice of life," she burns out quickly and is unable to sustain the energy needed to finish the course set before her.

Then he contrasted Sarah's approach to Daniel's. Gary compared him to a marathon runner, who is slow and steady, someone who takes his time and is hesitant to move forward too quickly. He tends to travel behind everyone else in the short run, but he's trying to strategically conserve energy for later. He's testing the course to see if it's worth running, which makes his decision making much more deliberative. Although he holds the attributes of wisdom and caution, his downfall can be that he moves too slowly, thus falling behind and unable to maximize the opportunities set before him.

As Gary drew out these insights about Sarah and Daniel with thoughtful question asking, one by one, everyone at the table locked into their conversation. It went on for about forty-five minutes, and every person at the table just listened because they were so interested in how Gary had steered the conversation intentionally toward self-discovery and self-analysis. He quickly uncovered unique facets of their personhood, and this immediately made them more interesting to the entire group at the table.

Even though he had just met them that day and knew virtually nothing about them, everything he said resonated with their relationship, personality types, and personhood. He highlighted some of their relational strengths and weaknesses and helped Sarah and Daniel realize things about themselves they had not previously been able to put into words. This happened to be their core misunderstanding about each other, the cause of much of their conflict, and the primary reason their relationship wasn't moving forward. Gary was able not just to find what was interesting about them and draw it out but to discover the distinctness about Sarah and Daniel quickly. Doing this reveals a true relational genius at work.

Gary knew how to zero in so that the people he had just met would feel known by him. He wanted them to sense his genuine curiosity and interest. When they did, it changed the dynamics of the conversation for the better. And he went about it in a way that didn't leave them feeling uncomfortably exposed, rather they were seen and understood for who they truly are. Gary could have simply let them talk about the dating relationship or kept it safe and predictable, allowing the dialogue to drift wherever it would go. But he decided to steer it through question asking and appropriate insights, which contributed to a more significant lunch experience than anyone expected. As a result, every friend of ours who was there wished they could have been the ones being observed and guided by Gary's insight. He showed interest in a way that drew everyone around the table to him, simply from the power of making others feel known.

We are simple creatures in this way. When we sense that someone gets us, it draws us out, similarly to a turtle coming out of its hard shell. We are too often tempted to remain under a hard exterior to protect ourselves. However, there is a part of us, probably the most important part, lying cautiously within; it is the part of our personhood that's soft and tender, even fragile. We want to be seen, but many people only bring that part of themselves out of their shell when someone takes the time to care and does so genuinely and lovingly. Knowing someone's personhood is crucial to making others feel understood.

Discovering Core Beliefs

Gary focused more on the personality aspect of personhood, more on how Sarah and Daniel were wired, and how that manifested in their relational world. But there are also other key arenas when it comes to discovering personhood, including discovering someone's core beliefs. Much of what people are about stems from the beliefs that drive them, which could involve their worldview, their spiritual convictions, and their personal core values. The path to understanding a person often begins with looking at what fuels the person internally. People's values drive their life choices; what kind of relationships they engage in; where they give time, money, and energy; how they treat people; and even how they wish to be treated. This undercurrent of beliefs has an enormous impact on how people's lives are fleshed out. Relational geniuses hold up the prism to discover how and why someone's values and beliefs radiate in their life the way they do. Then, as they engage the dimensions of people's lives, they enhance the quality of their relational world because people are drawn to the pursuit of knowing and understanding the essence.

People's expressing their core values externally can happen in many ways, such as where people give their money or volunteer their time or what they talk most passionately about. These are simple mediums that can reveal what is most interesting about someone.

One night a group of my friends went out to dinner to celebrate a friend's birthday. There was one guy named Aaron, who was new to the group because he had just started dating one of our good friends, Jen. After dinner, the waitress handed me the bill, and the awkward tallying of who owes what began. As I tried to figure out what each of us owed to the restaurant, Aaron reached across the table as if he were looking to see his portion of the bill. He grabbed the bill out of my hand, and before I knew what was happening, he got up from the table and began heading toward the server to pay for the entire meal.

He knew the only way to get away with paying for everyone was to leave the table quickly and go pay before we could stop him. We all sat there stunned at this young guy who was new to the group and who barely knew most of us. He paid for everyone's dinner (and it wasn't cheap). When he returned to the table, of course everyone was amazed at his generosity. We all thanked him profusely, which is a normal and appropriate expression of appreciation. And "thank-you" is usually where the discussion about a generous act ends.

However, Cheri was curious to get to know Aaron and wanted to move beyond the obvious and kind gesture of gratitude to discover what was behind his actions. She intuitively knew that whatever it was would reveal a strong part of who Aaron was as a person. So she asked a very simple but thoughtful and open-ended question that no one else thought to ask: "I know generous people don't usually like to draw attention to themselves because that's not the kind of people they are, but because generosity is such a rare quality, do you mind telling me what motivates your generosity? People aren't usually generous for the sake of being generous, and there's almost always a story behind it." Cheri was asking what drove his actions, as she sought to understand an internal value that shaped who he was and what he believed about generosity and people.

I could see he was growing more comfortable with the question. He actually wanted to share, because the focus wasn't on the act but instead on who he was as a person. He went on to describe how he was raised with a strong value for not using money to make yourself look good, or just add more stuff to your life, but to use money to serve others and bring people joy through giving. He also shared how he could go the rest of his life without receiving a gift again but couldn't imagine life without giving gifts to others, because that's what fills him with joy. That night, we didn't discover everything about Aaron, but in a brief moment we were able to catch a glimpse of one of his greatest life values. As a result, we understood his personhood far more than if Cheri had never asked that question.

There are opportunities before us all the time with the people we interact with. If we want to become relational geniuses, we must learn to capitalize on the moments when we see people's values being lived out. Where people spend what is valuable to them (time, money, passionate dialogue) is where you'll see what they value and believe; that's the cut of who they are, the reflective quality that shines through. Even in a short window of time, we can get a glimpse of someone's profound depth of personhood.

> If we want to become relational geniuses, we must learn to capitalize on the moments when we see people's values being lived out.

QUESTIONS TO ASK ABOUT PERSONHOOD

When it comes to drawing out the personhood of others, people don't usually even ask questions in this arena. Here are examples of the type of questions you can ask to zero in on someone's personhood, and as a result, increase your RI.

EXAMPLE 1

When you see someone give of himself in some way (through an act of generosity, showing compassion to someone in need, or treating an ordinary person with respect and dignity), ask, "What motivates you to do that?"

EXAMPLE 2

To discover a deeper dimension of someone's personhood, you could ask, "How do your spiritual convictions inform your decision making?" or "How would you describe the best parts of your personality?"

Exploring Sacred Stories

We must develop a taste for exploring new territory in people's lives. Then, as we cultivate it as an authentic desire we can learn to engage the layered facets of human beings that are most profoundly unique about them. If we want to do this with the hundreds of people we interact with throughout our lives, and if we want to help people feel genuinely known faster, with more precision and intentionality, we must start by focusing on others instead of ourselves. Then we must cultivate the ability to steer conversation toward greater depth, using

> Leaders who take time to get to know what is most sacred about people will also be invited to have the most sacred kind of influence in people's life.

the transformational art of good question asking. As a result, people will be more compelled to engage in our movement and mission.

Certainly it will take practice and repetition, along with trial and error, but people follow leaders for the long haul because they feel known by them. People tend to follow the leaders who see and value what is most distinct about their dreams, life story, and personhood. Leaders who take time to get to know what is most sacred about people will also be invited to have the most sacred kind of influence in people's life.

To develop our relational genius, we must redefine what it means to be interested in people and begin to discover the story their lives are telling. Again, the goal is not to be interested in every detail of people's lives but to discover what's most interesting about them and draw it out. When we begin to interact with people in these ways, we stop just wanting 101-level interactions; we don't want to be the receiver of them, nor the giver. Once we realize and experience that there's so much more territory to explore about someone's multifaceted humanness, and that it can often be done in a relatively short amount of time, we desire more of it. Once we realize that it can enhance the quality of our relationships, and enhance our leadership effectiveness, we will strive to give and receive more of it. If we keep working on this, we'll keep getting better at it. People are like walking novels, and there is great mystery within them waiting to be discovered.

The Energy Carrier

Energy is the fundamental currency of high
performance.

—*Jim Loehr and Tony Schwartz,*
The Power of Full Engagement

There are two kinds of people in the world: those who are able to read the tone and those who are able to set the tone. It's the difference between being a thermometer that measures the temperature and being a thermostat that sets the temperature. A relational genius has made the shift from being a tone reader to a tone setter.

Have you ever wondered how that certain leader whom you admire is able to lead with such force of presence and clarity? Have you ever noticed how that coworker of yours can relate to others in such a way that she virtually alters people's moods? Have you ever been curious as to how that friend of yours can single-handedly change the vibe of a room? Have you ever envied how easy these people make it look, yet how they do it still remains a mystery to you?

Though it may seem elusive as to how people set the tone, it comes down to one thing: *energy*.

The Power of Energy Carriers

We all have the capacity to be tone setters because we are all carriers of energy. Energy carriers bear an intangible yet potent source of power that originates from within them. What we choose to do with our internal energy determines how we affect our outer world of relationships. In essence, we can use our inner energy to affect the outer energy—meaning, the tone of our environment, the vibe of a room, the mood of people, and the overall feel of a setting.

> We can use our inner energy to affect the outer energy—meaning, the tone of our environment, the vibe of a room, the mood of people, and the overall feel of a setting.

Relational geniuses know how to identify and harness their internal power to affect outer change. They do this in order to set the tone, not only in their relational sphere but also in their leadership contexts. One single person can affect a large number of people, because they've learned to use the power on the inside to affect their potential impact on the outside. This is a choice that every leader must make and a skill they must develop. It's something we can all improve on as we strive to become relational geniuses who expand our influence.

In the presence of the best energy carriers, the energy of a room changes. They embody this in team settings, in large group environments, at staff meetings, and in other leadership or relational contexts. When they're absent, people sense the lack of energy. However, when they're present the mood of the environment comes alive. This capacity originates from the choice that leaders make to use their energy to enhance their current context. Relational geniuses have mastered the ability to do this, and so can you.

The Undercurrent of Energy

To become a relationally intelligent leader who has the ability to affect the tone of an entire room, it is essential to begin developing a specific skill set. To start with, we must learn how to accurately assess the tone of a given context. Then we must learn how to use relational intelligence to appropriately change that tone among the people we work with, serve alongside, and team up with; the audiences we speak to; and the movements we're trying to create. If we're unable to do this, we become *victims of our setting* rather than *changers of our setting*.

By being implementers of this kind of change, we are not trying to manipulate others or control a situation; rather, we're using our energy to make a positive contribution and enhance the relational quality of the environment we find ourselves in. Manipulation would involve fighting for control in order to serve ourselves or advance our own agenda above the good of the whole. But being an energy carrier is far from manipulation; it is way more about harnessing our energy to serve people as we seek to enhance their lives and relationships.

As leaders, there's almost always an opportunity to change our environment for the better, but this is a challenge that's often overlooked or even discounted. Countless times, I've seen people attempting to lead a group but fail to do so because the undercurrent of the group's energy is stronger than their own. Sometimes they can't even identify the dynamics of a room, and as a result they remain unable to change the environment. To be able to shift the undercurrent of a given situation in a better direction, our leadership must have force and strength behind it. Leadership without this component is leadership without influence.

If you have not been able to take your leadership to the next level and wonder what may be missing, assessing how you deal with the intangible but potent power of energy might provide a solution. Our energy, or lack thereof, affects our catalytic efforts, our ability to set transformation into motion, our strength of presence, our capacity to engage with our surroundings, and even our reputation among those we're trying to lead. If you want to become a better energy carrier and be able to harness this potent power within you, you must learn to overcome two energy killers and generate two energy catalysts.

Energy Killers

We've discussed what setting the tone is; now we need to turn to what hinders our ability to change the tone in any context. The obstacles for tone setters to overcome are called energy killers. The first energy killer is the appearance of alertness, and the second is distraction. To maximize the impact of our relational and leadership energy, we must learn how to overcome these two killers.

Energy Killer One: The Appearance of Alertness

The energy we carry within, and the force of its strength, is determined by how alert we are internally. It is entirely possible to appear highly alert on the outside, while being virtually asleep on the inside. Some people have mastered the art of looking engaged while in reality remaining completely disengaged. If we only acquire the skill of appearing alert, we fail to be attuned to our surroundings, thus relinquishing our opportunity to be agents of change of its tone. Sometimes we grow lazy at being attentive to our environment, and as a result we turn off our radar to the needs and opportunities around us. The true source of our lack of ability to be a dynamic force of change is often related to this problem of internal sleepiness.

> The energy we carry within, and the force of its strength, is determined by how alert we are internally.

Some leaders have bought into the belief that if they appear alert this will carry the energy required to lead others effectively.

They think they can go on autopilot internally, and that their external appearance will be enough to lead effectively. Maybe you have been on the receiving end of someone who is internally asleep. Have you ever been in a conversation, and at some point, you realize the other person is not absorbing what you're saying? He may appear externally alert, but in actuality, he's checked out internally. At best, he's acting as though he is listening. When my wife catches me doing this, she stops and asks me, "Do you know what I mean?" I give a casual, "Of course." Then to test me, "OK, then tell me what I just said." I always fail because she knows me all too well.

Forgetfulness

If you wonder how to gauge your own internal alertness, one sign is revealed in your forgetfulness. What seem to be situations and encounters that are meaningful enough for others to remember, you have a tendency to forget. If you were internally alert, you would be able to better remember because you were actually paying full attention.

When leaders lack this level of attentiveness, they tend to build a reputation as being forgetful. I'm not referring to forgetting incidental details, but rather a forgetfulness that may be the result of daydreaming for part or all of a conversation that is important. This happens in informal social contexts as well as more formal work settings.

> If you wonder how to gauge your own internal alertness, one sign is revealed in your forgetfulness.

For instance, you may have a staff member who's talked to you several times about the same issue (she is unsure of how her success at work is measured, or she wants clarity on job responsibilities, or she discussed with you a concern she has with one of the team members). Maybe you appear to be engaged with her in conversation initially, and the staff member thinks you understand in a way that causes you to take action to resolve the issue. But because you are actually not alert internally, you don't truly absorb what issue she is trying to get resolved. Therefore you don't take the anticipated action.

At some point, the staff person realizes you haven't fully grasped what she said because nothing is being done. That's what causes her to keep coming back to you with the same issue. This traces back to an outer appearance that communicates you're listening and will take action, but at the same time, you lack internal alertness and remain mostly unaware of the importance of what the staff member is sharing with you. This RI principle transfers into social settings, personal relationships, and leadership contexts.

At times, I've made this mistake because I've placed value on making people feel listened to by the external appearance of my face, body language, and even outer responsiveness to them. Although those things can be good to do as basic relational skills, they remain incomplete. Being awake on the outside yet asleep on the inside isn't going to help you become a great tone setter . . . or a relational genius.

One person who doesn't let me off the hook without completing the picture is my wife, Cheri (and I'm so glad she doesn't). Unfortunately, she's had to revisit certain subjects with me multiple times when she thought they were resolved because of how alert I *appeared to be* at the time of the conversation. As time elapsed, she realized that I hadn't absorbed what was discussed enough to remember the outcome of our conversation. Sometimes I don't even recall having the conversation at all (sorry, Cheri).

When we were dating, we initially talked about having a family in the future. She shared how important it was for her to stay home from working as a nurse so that she could devote herself to raising our kids. I was supportive and told her I thought that was a good decision for us. Soon after we got married, the subject came up again.

In that second conversation, I asked her if she wanted to work full-time or part-time when we had kids. She looked at me with squinting, curious eyes, as if she weren't sure I was being serious, wondering if I remembered our previous conversation. I wasn't asking because I secretly wanted her to work. I had simply forgotten about our previous conversation. She was surprised at my memory lapse, first, because this was so important to her, and second, because I had appeared to be listening the first time. She thought we had brought closure to this decision and that I realized how much it meant to her, but this clearly wasn't the case.

A few years into our marriage, we started preparing to have kids very soon. You're not going to believe it, but I actually forgot again (please don't judge me). By round three she was pretty disheartened because she thought I was not listening, didn't care, or I secretly wanted her to work. To her, that's why I kept bringing it up. In actuality, it was none of these options. In our two previous conversations, I had essentially been taking a mental nap while maintaining an absorbed countenance. I wasn't engaging the conversation with internal alertness, and it was now damaging our relationship.

Sometimes I've had to learn the hard way, but remaining internally alert is not an option when it comes to showing up in our lives and showing up for other people. What we miss in the process is too important to the relationships in our lives, not to mention in leadership contexts. We'll begin to kill our impact of contributing to the outer energy around us if we allow internal sleepiness to become an ongoing habit.

Waking Up on the Inside

I've seen the appearance of alertness kill energy in many leadership contexts. Drew is one leader I know who showed this dynamic in his relational world and in his leadership endeavors. No matter where he was or what he was doing, he appeared to be alert on the outside. Plus, he gave fully of his time and commitment, and he always prepared for what he was leading. But I made two observations that revealed his lack of internal alertness. He would consistently fail to remember things we discussed (forgetfulness), and he consistently failed to carry the energy when it came to leading a larger number of people in groups or teams. In my observation, he didn't know why.

I saw this clearly through one of his leadership responsibilities, which involved speaking at leadership training workshops to medium-sized groups of fifty to a hundred people. I had seen other leaders in this venue carry the energy quite well. They were able to set the tone they desired in the room. But even though Drew was talented and likeable and had some extraordinary leadership skills that came out in certain contexts, he was unable to establish a strong presence and create a tone in the room for effective learning, authentic engagement, and genuine interest from the crowd. This contrasted with other leaders who could control the tone of the crowd as a skilled vocalist could control the voice when singing. Singers knew where they wanted to drive the energy, and they did it.

Drew is an example of someone who focused on developing the skills of working hard, likeability, and offering his time and talents, but he didn't invest in his internal world of energy. He was awake on the outside but lacked alertness on the inside. As a result, he wasn't accurately attuned to the dynamics of the crowd and therefore didn't know how to set the tone in a room.

After noticing him walking away confused as to why he wasn't able to establish the same level of engagement as other leaders were, I pulled him aside one day to share what I observed.

As I gave him feedback, I saw that he didn't even realize when the crowd lost interest, nor did he sense any disengagement from the people in the room. As I shared my observations with him, it seemed he was the only person in the room who wasn't aware of his lack of internal energy. Most people who are relationally intelligent in this capacity will change how they lead when the tone is not what they want to be creating. But Drew seemed to keep going, just as he had been, not attuned to the vibe of the crowd. As we discussed how he could increase his level of internal alertness, he recognized that he had been working from the assumption that as long as he was physically present with his energy, it would automatically set the tone he desired. But as we talked I knew he got it when he said, "Maybe I've been taking mental naps while being physically awake."

The irony here is that we sometimes put so much effort into our external, physical energy that we fail to pay proper attention to our internal energy. Though this effort could be a great strength, if we neglect staying internally alert, it can be a great weakness in leadership. To improve in this arena, we must continue to pay attention to how alert we are on the inside, because the more awake we are internally the greater impact potential we'll have in the environments all around us.

> The irony here is that we sometimes put so much effort into our external, physical energy that we fail to pay proper attention to our internal energy.

Energy Killer Two: Distraction

A second major killer to maximizing our internal energy is distraction. It's the thief that steals our energy. When we are distracted internally, we emit a distracted energy externally. Many of us run from setting to setting, rattled with loud distractions that no one hears except us. Our string of thoughts are clinging to our mind, while we're simultaneously attempting to be present in our environment. But the more we allow ourselves to be distracted, the more tiring it becomes to arrange the myriad thoughts and remain attuned to our outer world. Relational geniuses have learned not to underestimate the power of distraction when it comes to tone setting around them.

I see this dynamic play out firsthand in my own life. It has always been a battle for me to fight distraction, and as a result bring clarity to my inner life. But for a long time I never made the connection between distraction and a lack of impact in my leadership. One of the greatest mediums in which we can hope to set the tone is with a large audience, because there is room for great influence in large numbers. From the time I began speaking, I have always tried to work hard to develop good content and to be fully prepared so I was able to deliver my talk well; I tried to seek feedback afterward to improve my communication skills for the next time. Even though I consistently gave solid effort, I found that after I walked off the stage something still seemed to be missing. I'd do all I knew to prepare, yet I sensed that I hadn't effectively reached my audience to the degree I knew was possible.

As a speaker, I'm usually able to sense and assess the vibe of the crowd. I can tell when I'm losing them, when they get bored, or when they remain unmoved; I've had a lot of practice and experience. But despite being able to gauge my audience's tone, the challenge to change it remains. As I discussed this dilemma one day with Cheri, she offered an insight that dramatically shifted my approach to speaking. Although the words coming out my mouth were well prepared and connected, and though I was engaged by all appearances, I was not what she called "centered." In her analysis, I was distracted.

Her hope in sharing this was to remind me that my best moments on stage were those when I was "fully there." Instead of being distracted or scattered, I need to improve on remaining fully present. Cheri suggested that I clear my mind and heart before stepping onto any stage. She encouraged me to bring all of who I am—and therein would lie my greatest impact. Although I continue to grow in this quest, when I am successful at doing this I notice a significant difference in how I'm able to shift the undercurrent of energy in a crowd and increase my impact. This happens best when I feed the force of my own internal energy. I'm able to remove the killer of distraction when I remain centered.

From Centered to Allness

When we're centered, we're able to bring the *allness* of who we are to our present moment, which enables us to become better energy carriers and enhances the quality of our relationships. Jesus dealt with the idea of allness when confronted with the question of the greatest commandment. He refers to allness as it relates to the powerful force of loving God and others in relationships. He wraps the idea of allness into four realms as He challenges humanity to give the fullness of themselves through their heart, soul, mind, and strength. You may be familiar with His declaration in the Gospel of Mark:

> Love the LORD your God with all your heart and with all your soul and with all your mind and with all your strength. The second is this: Love your neighbor as yourself. There is no commandment greater than these.[1]

Above all else, Jesus' desire for each one of us is to embody the fullness of love with the entirety of who we are. If we don't, we begin to compartmentalize who we are, thus allowing parts of ourselves to remain disconnected and thus *distracted* from who and what is right in front of us. Jesus understood that when we fail to integrate our complete self, we fragment the impact of our energy.

> Jesus understood that when we fail to integrate our complete self, we fragment the impact of our energy.

Be All There

In the original Greek language of the New Testament, Jesus uses the preposition *ek*, which means "from the center." Then he connects *ek* with *holos*, which means "the parts are all present" or "none are missing." Jesus uses these two words together four times to emphasize His desire for human beings to love God *from the center* of our being, bringing the allness of who we are, that is, every part of ourselves into that relationship. Jesus was heightening the importance of what I believe is a critical principle of relational intelligence: *wherever you are, be all there*. He's trying to help us understand the connection between living fully present and the holistic experience of love.

When we're centered in the present with God, we experience His power in profound ways. In essence, that power creates a charge within. This charge is the intangible force that creates impact outside of us. We ought not seek this power for power's sake; rather our motive in seeking it is to please God as we find our strength in Him. When every part of our being is fully present, we offer our whole selves to whatever we're doing. Our undivided attention becomes focused in the moment, on the task at hand, or on the people involved, thus empowering our ability to set the tone. This not only enhances the quality of our relationships but paves the path toward fueling our inner energy to more effectively influence our external world.

In my attempt to deepen my impact and bring my allness to life, here are some reflective questions that I use to center myself and prepare to set the tone effectively. Sometimes this happens in extended time, but mostly it happens in brief moments. Reflecting on these questions keeps me centered in who I want to be and where I want to go. It guides me to bring my whole self into the present moment of my relational sphere.

Heart: *What's the condition of my heart?*

> Do my desires reflect what I want the essence of my heart to be?
>
> Do I feel weighed down with fear or other negative emotions?
>
> Do any of my emotions drain others, or have any become unhealthy, even toxic?
>
> Does my heart feel free to be fully present in the moments I find myself in?

Soul: *What's the condition of my soul?*

Is my personhood rooted in the right things?

In whom (or what) do I find my greatest worth?

Is my soul centered in God and at rest with Him?

Am I able to remain still in God's presence and find my identity in Him?

Mind: *What's the condition of my mind?*

What is the content of my thoughts?

Am I bogged down with anxious, confusing, and distracted thoughts?

Is my mind filled with clarity, peace, and wisdom?

Is my mind engaged in what's right in front of me (or is it somewhere else)?

Strength: *What's the condition of my physical strength?*

Am I treating my body well, or have I neglected to foster good health?

Am I getting enough rest, or am I fatigued and worn down?

Am I giving my best effort to what I've set out to do?

Have I been honoring God with my time and effort lately?

As we reflect on these dimensions of our personhood, the process of centering ourselves results in integrating all dimensions together so that we are functioning synergistically and with great strength of presence. We're not always able to be completely centered in the sense that every part of ourselves is 100 percent healthy and perfectly aligned with who we desire to be, but being centered is never about achieving internal perfection. Rather, it's about understanding where we are in an authentic and honest way, and then continuously striving to bring the allness of ourselves to God and to others. As we attempt to offer our best, we can pray that our lives are a gift to God and to those around us.

Energy Catalysts

If remaining internally alert and centered is not in place, we will be unable to generate the catalysts necessary to activate our greatest leadership impact. By *catalyst*, I mean something that is a change agent. There is an invisible yet powerful undercurrent that can be shifted if we implement these energy catalysts. Becoming an effective energy catalyst is what helps us move the power we have on the inside to create change on the outside. Now that we've discussed the two energy killers, let's turn our attention to a couple of energy catalysts that can launch us toward becoming leaders who change the mood of a crowd, environment, or conversation.

Energy Catalyst One: Externalizing Your Internal Energy

Sueann is a friend of mine with an uncanny ability to generate energy in any context she enters. Whether it's a leadership environment, a social context, or some other relational sphere, she knows how to harness the energy within her to change the energy around her. Her relational genius is revealed when she merges the inner and outer worlds in order to set the tone. I've witnessed her doing this on multiple occasions. By virtue of her presence, she changes the energy; she's a true energy carrier.

Recently, I asked her how she does it. In our conversation, she agreed that it first requires internal alertness and centeredness, and she attributed her staying attuned to her environment to this. But what she said next really intrigued me: "You have to want to change the atmosphere bad enough in order to intentionally make it happen. It takes effort to offer the best of yourself to generate a charge of energy in the setting around you."

Another way she externalizes her internal energy is to believe she has something to positively contribute that will improve the mood of an environment and the people around her. If we don't have confidence that we have something important to offer, then we won't consistently take the action required to set the tone. Along with confidence, Sueann also described how it takes assertiveness (but without being too pushy) to influence this invisible dynamic in a given context. It takes assertiveness because we're taking the solitary power from within us and attempting to envelop a group of people, or even a large audience, into it—which requires tremendous effort.

Recognizing how to better contribute to an existing atmosphere involves identifying where the deficit of energy is. This could be seen in a group that's bored or disengaged, one that's frustrated or cynical, or one that's exhausted or just lacking connectedness. Every leader has the ability to take what's inside and help close that gap of negativity to change the energy of a room. Energy carriers see the deficit in a given situation, and instead of falling into it, they carry people out of it.

> Energy carriers see the deficit in a given situation, and instead of falling into it, they carry people out of it.

One way Sueann does this is seen in how she leads a meeting. She happens to be an event coordinator, so she's constantly working with various teams of staff and volunteers. On one occasion, while leading a planning meeting, she saw that her team members were tired and disconnected from each other. To counteract the tiredness, she was able to externalize her internal energy with enthusiasm and excitement to help lift the mood. When she saw that her team was feeling disconnected, she changed her agenda. Instead of moving right to the tasks and agenda of the meeting, she asked each person to share something personal that is going on in his or her life. It started slowly, as if no one really wanted to share, but Sueann persevered by asking thoughtful, personal questions. She was also responsive and affirming about the honesty of what people shared. Though simple in concept, as people opened up it changed the whole environment of the room. As the conversation unfolded, it fostered a sense of cohesion among the team, and as a result, Sueann successfully changed the tone of disconnectedness to connectedness. The meeting became more fun and soon more productive; it was full of *energy*.

When moments like this occur, leaders have to be ready for them, even if it means changing the agenda to take time to create an experience where the energy in the room is enhanced. Leaders can often remain so task-oriented that they disconnect from assessing the energy in the room and therefore miss an opportunity for positive impact with their teams. Sometimes these leaders are tone-deaf, and for them they must continue to pay attention and learn to read the unspoken mood of people in a room.

Sueann's relational genius is also revealed when she's informally leading in a social context. If she sees that the group lacks vibrancy, she'll inject just enough of a jolt to generate a charge of energy and bring the group to life. She does this with relational intelligence, not pushing people away by shocking them so much that they're confused or feel threatened. Instead, she intrigues and pulls them as a result of externalizing her energy. When I asked her how she does this, she described it as "tearing down predictable walls to create a spark."

When a group conversation is dull and Sueann needs to create a jolt, she often asks a provocative question that she knows will be interesting to that specific group of people. One time, we were with some friends who she knew were all passionate about their beliefs yet happened to be very tired and disengaged at the moment. To create a spark, she asked a simple yet thought-provoking question: "Do you guys think it's more important to be kind or to be right?" This was her attempt to *tear down the walls of predictability*. She went on to share her own opinion, which was strong but also inviting of their input. As a result, she was able to generate vibrant dialogue and completely change the tone of the group. It rapidly went from tired to awake, from bored to interested, and from meaningless to relevant.

It would be a mistake to try generating this energy cata-lyst only in medium-size or large group settings because we can develop this ability in increments from small to big. In other words, if we can't affect the energy among one or two people in an informal setting, how can we do it with two to three hundred people, or in larger leadership contexts? One way we can begin developing this aspect of relational intelligence is by practicing it in the small moments of our everyday lives; this can culmi-nate in greater impact as our future unfolds.

In summary of these observations, here are five ways to gen-erate the energy catalyst of externalizing your internal energy:

1. Begin by intentionally wanting to change a negative tone.
2. Know you have something positive to contribute to enhance the atmosphere.
3. Be assertive with how you externalize your energy.
4. Tear down predictable walls to create a spark.
5. Practice carrying the energy within a variety of contexts, but start with individuals and in smaller groups.

When it comes to making an impact, sometimes we need to change the context for the better. Other times the context is already positive, and we simply need to contribute whatever good we can. If we desire to be effective energy carriers who set the tone, we must know the goal of the tone that we want to set and then strive to drive the conversation toward that end. It takes RI to do it right, but when we do, it's a gift to the people in every environment we step into.

Energy Catalyst Two: Capitalize on the Moment

My friend Hank can change the tone of his environment as well as almost anyone I know. He can make a small gathering or ordinary moment feel like a monumental event, simply through the energy he brings to it. He also carries this power of presence when he speaks to large audiences. One of our mutual mentors linked Hank's capacity to affect such change to his ability to capitalize on a moment. Essentially, he was describing Hank's ability to see the power of what seems like an ordinary encounter to others but in actuality is filled with the extraordinary. To him, a given moment can teach a life lesson, reveal a remarkable mystery, capture the essence of beauty, or remind us why we're alive. If we can see the significance in what appears to be mundane, we can recognize the weight of that meaning at an internal place and then share the power of it with our surrounding environment. This phenomenon changes the energy around us dramatically and enhances our ability to lead through relationship. This is an effective energy catalyst for a relational genius.

Capitalizing on the moment is not about conjuring up pseudo-meaning out of a meaningless occurrence, nor is it even about seeing something extraordinary in the ordinary. That would only fuel a false sense of reality and leave us projecting an unrealistic view of the world around us. This leads to individuals or crowds seeing us as irrelevant and out of touch with what is true and real. Instead, we must lean into the moments of life that are pulsating strongly within them while remaining hidden, just enough to be missed by the person who's not looking for them. That's often how the greatest moments in life arise. It's not that they're disguised, but they're often tucked behind a mysterious veil, which calls us to seek further, search harder, and feel deeper. Generating this energy catalyst often involves recognizing what's inherently extraordinary but could be masked in the ordinary, and thus overlooked by most.

When we engage this quest to see the magic behind seemingly ordinary moments, we'll find a whole new part of us coming alive, thus injecting that vibrant force of energy into the settings around us. Instead of people thinking we are somehow exaggerating what exists in a moment, they'll resonate with a sense of wonder at how in sync we are with something profoundly alive and true right in front of us. Capitalizing on a moment is the gift that we can bring to others, and a reminder that there are extraordinary moments of life pulsating all around us.

As human beings, we long to see the wonder, the meaning, and the power in our everyday lives, but somehow it eludes us more than we'd like. If someone is able to share the ability to capitalize on life's magnificent moments, it gives us hope that we can do the same. If we learn to navigate this aspect of relational intelligence, we'll develop an ability to change the energy in a room faster and deeper than we ever thought we could. We will learn how to create a visceral response and move people forward in what they desire for their lives. This can happen through a one-on-one encounter, a smaller group setting, or a one-on-many larger audience experience.

> When we engage this quest to see the magic behind seemingly ordinary moments, we'll find a whole new part of us coming alive, thus injecting that vibrant force of energy into the settings around us.

Seizing the Now Moments

The opportunity to capitalize on a moment comes in a variety of ways, but there are two that occur frequently. The first shows itself when we're experiencing something mystical or significant. We miss it if we are not fully present to pay attention at the time, or if we are present but we miss the significance of what is passing right in front of us. Either way, this moment is before us and we must decide if we're going to recognize it and then know what to do in the situation to capitalize on it. This first step begins by looking for moments like these, as they emerge right before our eyes.

Hank is always on the lookout for these meaning-laced encounters, no matter where he is or what he's doing. On one occasion, he radically changed the energy of the crowd when he was speaking at our church by telling of a story that may at first appear normal but was filled with the extraordinary. While visiting San Francisco with some friends, he woke up early one morning and was looking for something to do while everyone else was asleep. He decided to go for a walk by himself through downtown to explore the city. He came to an intersection where he saw a large group of people and was curious about what was happening. He had stumbled upon a walkathon for breast cancer. As he observed the scene, a participant named Bertha walked up to him and initiated a conversation. She was an older woman with a quirky personality and a thick New York accent. It struck Hank as funny that she had a cigarette dangling from her mouth while walking to raise money for cancer research. But Hank was drawn to her.

Bertha took time to talk with him, and he was mildly fascinated by her idiosyncrasies. Then she asked Hank to walk with her to support the cause. At first he shrugged it off because it wasn't really what he came to do. Plus he felt the need to go find his friends. However, he sensed Bertha's passion for this cause as she tried to persuade him, so he gave in and began walking with her. Sharing the path with thousands of people whose convictions fueled their steps, Hank walked alongside Bertha as she shared her life story. What initially appeared to be an ordinary, even lonely, morning became one filled with laughter, connection with others, and a life lesson for Hank. He later described this as a "beautiful experience that he'd never forget."

Hank shared this story at church, along with the life lesson he learned. The mood in the audience was already beginning to shift from casual engagement to intrigued curiosity as he described it. Then he brought out the depth and richness of that life lesson he had learned. Hank explained how Bertha got him to walk a mile with her because she saw him when no one else did. She showed interest when everyone else was walking by, and she wooed him in with her kindness and charm. In essence, he followed her, and her cause, because she cared. Hank connected that experience to the truth that we can persuade others to walk with us just by caring. It was a simple truth, but it was charged with life and power. And the audience felt it. They were leaning in; everyone could feel the emotion swimming across the room.

This occurrence of catalyzing the energy of the moment was far from a manipulation, and not simply a result of Hank's charisma. It was the natural product of his ability to capitalize on a moment and then share the potency of the experience with those around him. This is what energy carriers do if they desire to be catalysts. As we grow in our ability to capitalize on everyday moments, we also grow in our capacity to change the energy around us through the weight those moments offer.

If we want to become relational geniuses, we must learn to transfer the richness and meaning of these encounters to our audience and those we're entrusted to lead—whether it's in a one-on-one context, a small group setting, or a large crowd. As a result, our impact will be greater, and the quality of the relationships in our lives will be enhanced. Every one of us has the ability to create energy by capitalizing on moments and sharing the power behind their mystery with others.

Seizing the Emerging Moments

Along with the ability to capitalize on moments that aren't seen by others, there are also emerging moments that everyone recognizes, but most don't know what to do with them. This is when something clearly meaningful is happening right in front of us. These moments are not hidden or behind a mysterious veil; rather, they are begging for us to seize them with the right kind of energy. If we allow them to pass us by, we lose a great opportunity to catalyze the energy of our leadership impact.

I was at our annual Christmas party for our two-year interns at Mosaic, whom we call *protégés*. They move to Los Angeles from all over the world to serve and learn at Mosaic for a couple years and attain their master's degree in global leadership. It's an intense developmental experience that can be life-changing for them because of the tremendous amount of heart and effort they put into it. Every year at our Christmas party, we have a brief time of Q & A, which usually proves to be a thought-provoking and interesting experience, not necessarily an emotional one.

On this occasion, there was a significant undercurrent emerging as the protégés began to spontaneously share their feelings about the program that ended for them in six months. It seemed they were all in a similar place of looking to process their feelings around this very defining season of their lives. The tone of sadness blended with the joy of accomplishment, was virtually screaming at me. I recognized that I could do one of two things. I could allow the undercurrent to drift wherever it might go and risk losing the chance to guide these protégés to where they were longing to go but didn't know how to get there. Or I could seize the opportunity before me to lean into this emerging energy and bring it to its fullest capacity of strength and impact.

I sensed that they needed to adequately process among each other the seeds of sorrow planted within them. And I knew they needed someone to help them experience this together so they could let go of this season of life in a healthy way, while remaining able to absorb the great joy that it brought at the same time. So I proceeded to explain that very thing to them. In a way, it gave them permission to start grieving over the closing of this amazing chapter of their lives so they would be able to celebrate the beginning of a new one.

In this moment, I shared how much they all meant to me, and how they had experienced change in their own lives that had deeply affected my life as well. The energy began to shift from one of wandering emotion to clarity of heart and even immense gratitude. They knew what they had to do to begin processing, and their feelings were acknowledged, even honored. Plus, there was a burden lifted from the room while the power of the moment was strengthened and brought to the light. In that situation, it may seem like it was the obvious route to take, but I know that I've missed chances like this on countless occasions, to take charge and capitalize on moments. When richness of emotion, strength of thought, and communal energy around a specific longing emerge right before my eyes, I often fail to seize the moment that has emerged. But this time I didn't. Instead, I didn't allow it to taper off or eventually vanish; I sought to capitalize on the potential for great impact so it wouldn't be lost.

This kind of impact causes people to remember with uncanny clarity the experiences that potentially shape their lives, that help remind them of profound truths, or that guide them toward completing the course of emotion in a given season of life. These are the extraordinary moments of life that we remember and treasure as human beings. They are the intersections of deep impact. To be leaders striving for relational intelligence, we must capitalize on them with greater frequency and quality as we strive to become relational geniuses who cultivate relational health all around us. But to make this happen, we must change how we interact with our surrounding environments and learn to better capitalize on moments.

The Gift of Energy

Being effective energy carriers requires us to understand that . . .

The more we maintain internal alertness,

The more we center ourselves in the present,

The more we embrace the invitation of allness,

The more we externalize the internal energy within,

The more we capitalize on life's meaningful moments,

then the more we will take the strength that's growing within and use it to change the energy around us for the better, leaving the people in our lives and the atmosphere we find ourselves in more enriched, alive, and *energized*.

5

The Compelling Relator

What lies behind us and what lies before us are
tiny matters compared to what lies within us.

—*Ralph Waldo Emerson*[1]

Boredom is a rampant epidemic in our culture. The results
of boredom are everywhere, and especially revealed in
how we interact with technology.[2]

- If someone visits a Web site and stays for fifteen seconds or
  longer, experts consider that a successful visit.

- If a person goes to a Web site, and after clicking three times
  doesn't find what he or she is looking for, studies show that
  it's highly unlikely the person will stay.

- If a Web site address is more than seven letters, people are
  five times less likely to type it in—because "it takes too
  long."

Think about how crazy this is: people lose interest if they have to click four times to get what they're looking for. People are unwilling to focus their attention long enough to type eight letters of a URL. If their attention is engaged on a Web site for just fifteen seconds, it's a win.

Thanks to this all pervasive condition, the role of television advertising has shifted as well. It has become primarily about giving consumers control of what they want. DVR and TiVo allow us to fast-forward through commercials we don't want to watch or even parts of TV shows that are not interesting. In a study done by CNN, researchers experimented with a thirty-second newsflash to provide "more in-depth coverage." They discovered that thirty seconds was "too long for the viewer." In fact, they found that most viewers' attention span preferred a seven-second newsflash. Example after example reveals that we live in a culture whose interests is increasingly difficult to capture. Whatever doesn't engage our interest quickly enough is rapidly getting cut out of our lives.

People want everything faster, better, and more interesting because people get bored more quickly and easily than ever before. This is the generation we live in. Although this reality is revealed through how we interact with technology, I think the arena of life that's affected most is our relationships.

The Strength of Boredom

Recently, one of my favorite talk show hosts discussed his own experience of this cultural reality and how it affected his relational world. As he shared part of his life journey, he described how easily he grew bored as a kid. At an early age, this was a weakness that arose among his friends. As a result, throughout his life he chose to take this weakness of becoming easily bored, learn from it, and become a more interesting person so that other people would not be bored with him. He knew what it felt like to be so easily bored, and he didn't want to be the cause of boredom to others.

For years, this value of becoming more interesting has pervaded every aspect of his life, his relationships, and even his career endeavors. It has motivated him take a self-identified weakness and use it to drive his pursuit of becoming the most interesting person he can be, which is now one of his great strengths. In his career ambitions, this led him to become a popular radio host who discusses everything from politics to philosophy to religion to relationships. Today, he consistently receives high ratings on his show, and thousands of people tune in every day to listen to him talk, because he refuses to be boring. As a result, he has become a person others want to listen to because he intentionally pursued becoming a more compelling person to others.

When I heard his story, I was reminded of the epidemic of boredom that exists in our culture. I thought of how many of us hold the value of becoming a compelling person, and how many others of us hold the value of relating to others well. But how many of us merge these two values so that we arrive at a place where we relate to others in a compelling way? How many of us are *compelling relators?*

When we realize how critical it is to cultivate the ability to engage people's interest in our relational spheres, we can begin to synergize our desires to be both compelling and relational. Too many people forgo these desires and, as a result, become boring as they neglect the intentional pursuit to become interesting. They subsequently forfeit the opportunity to increase their influence because they are unable to hold the attention of the people they are trying to relate to. This is where becoming a compelling relator intersects relational intelligence.

We could blame people for their short attention span or for becoming bored too easily, or, like this radio talk show host, we can be driven to become more interesting people in how we interact with others, which fosters RI and helps us cultivate relational vibrancy and health. We don't have to be victims of the epidemic of boredom. Instead, we can recognize the cultural reality that exists—that people get bored easily—and turn that weakness into the fuel that drives us toward developing the strength of becoming a more captivating person in our relational world.

Reverse Boredom

So, how does the epidemic of boredom that we see in our culture transfer into our relational world? Is it possible to bore people less in our relationships and engage them faster and better in conversation? What if we changed how we expressed our passions, altered how we communicated with others, and adjusted how we led meetings? What if we refused to be irrelevant to people? How much better could this engage people's interest and foster relational health and greater impact around us?

Imagine if this were a more developed value in certain arenas. How would it affect the education system? What if teachers worked harder to become more interesting to their students? What if they began to affect their students with more compelling learning methods, and through designing curriculum more creatively? In another arena, imagine if pastors in churches became less boring and irrelevant. What if they worked harder to compel their audience to seek something meaningful and stopped assuming that people are automatically interested simply because what they are saying is "true"? Imagine this happening at meetings at work, which are notoriously boring thanks to information overload and irrelevance (or maybe just a boring boss). What if employers and team leaders were determined to make their meetings more engaging and more compelling? Imagine if people in social circles became more compelling conversationalists, rather than frustrating people with less-than-stimulating dialogue?

Imagine if there were no such thing as being stuck in a conversation that you couldn't wait to get out of.

Although people tend to get easily bored, we must be careful not to assume that people don't have a strong capacity to pay attention. As leaders, we must take on our own responsibility to pursue becoming more compelling in our leadership, communication, and relationships. Maybe there's not just the epidemic of boredom out there, but an epidemic of "boring," meaning it's not just that people have a short attention span. We may not be interesting enough to hold their attention. We have the power to change this. Each of us has the ability to expand people's capacity to be attentive by learning how to relate to them in more compelling ways.

> Maybe there's not just the epidemic of boredom out there, but an epidemic of "boring."

Four Ways to Become a Compelling Relator

The simple truth is this: the more interesting we are as people, the more compelling we become as leaders. As we strive to become compelling relators, we will draw more people to our mission, accelerate momentum as we move with others toward a common cause, and synergistically create more dynamic energy and cohesion interpersonally. So if you want to increase your RI, here are four ways to become a more compelling relator.

> The simple truth is this: the more interesting we are as people, the more compelling we become as leaders.

Dare to Be Controversial When the Moment Calls for It

In his book *Tribes*, Seth Godin writes, "Heretics are the new leaders."[3] He isn't emphasizing theological heresy but declaring that leaders must challenge normal patterns of thinking. They must dare to be controversial. Relationally intelligent leaders don't try to please everyone, and they refuse to relinquish what they care about simply to make others happy. As a result, they encounter resistance because the majority of people resist change.

Jesus once said, "Beware when all people speak well of you."[4] If everyone always agrees with you, and if no one ever criticizes you, then you're probably not leading as much as you think. There's no doubt that leaders sometimes create controversy by leading from their convictions. An underlying fear could be what holds you back. Maybe it's fear of what others may think, fear of disappointing people, or fear of failure. If it's not fear that hinders your willingness to step into controversy, then maybe it's lack of clarity about your values, mission, and convictions. If everyone speaks well of you, you are giving in to the forces around you more than you are allowing the force from within you to emerge from the strength of who you are.

Although relational intelligence certainly involves the ability to create harmony and make peace, it also helps us realize when we need to be bold and controversial. As a leader, you will never maximize your effectiveness unless there are moments when you speak and act in a way that creates necessary and productive tension. It feels good when people agree with us, and we like it when our opinions are validated by others. In fact, most people feel more comfortable when their relationships are harmonious than when they are tense and filled with conflict. But the path of least resistance is not always the way to become a more compelling relator.

> As a leader, you will never maximize your effectiveness unless there are moments when you speak and act in a way that creates necessary and productive tension.

It takes RI to know how to get along well with others, but this shouldn't be done at the cost of standing up for a truth or conviction just because it may cause conflict and tension. People willing to take a stand for their beliefs, even when it's not the most popular decision, tend to increase their ability to be interesting to those around them (when it is done with relational intelligence). As a result, they earn the ears of others. The quest to become a relational genius involves developing this ability to discern when to courageously step into a moment and be boldly controversial. Of course this must be done for the right reasons and with the right motives, but it must be done. Doing this without RI has the reverse effect, and it repels people.

I recently led a team of twenty-five people to Zambia. Our team was especially excited about this trip because of the family that would be hosting and guiding us while we were there. Dan and his family lived in Zambia, and they hosted us for the two weeks while we were there. I was initially drawn to Dan when I first met him when he visited Los Angeles. He shared stories about his movie-like adventures in eight African nations. He had spent his entire life serving people in these countries and sharing the message of hope and love. We got to hear some of the incredible things he was accomplishing there, and we also noticed how innovative he was with carrying out his mission in Africa. But that was just the beginning.

After arriving in Zambia, our entire team was quickly inspired as we got to experience firsthand all that Dan had built through his leadership endeavors, from helping orphanages and launching an internet café to building a guest hotel, to funding other humanitarian projects and creating jobs, to a leadership school that trains and develops hundreds of indigenous entrepreneurs in Zambia. Not only had he built a layered empire of proactive, servant-hearted influencers, he had extreme strength of presence in the cities and communities he took us through.

You can probably already tell that he's an incredibly interesting person, but when he led a question-and-answer time with our team, we realized this to be even truer. Our team came with anticipation and curiosity about what he would say, because he had earned such credibility with what we had experienced with him already. He surpassed our expectations. As our team poured out questions, he gave one engaging answer after another. Then came the question that I'm sure every team asks him when they come on short-term trips to partner with him: "What can we do as Americans to help?"

We could see the tension creep slowly across Dan's face. He paused as we anxiously awaited his answer. He seemed almost annoyed at first glance; as he answered we realized it wasn't annoyance but more of a healthy, justified frustration. Dan shared how team after team predictably asks that very question, and indeed how the whole world seemed to be asking the question. But instead of feeling comforted and supported by our concern, he felt frustrated at how we were all missing the point. This is when the tension began to rise even further in the room. In this moment, it was clear we were asking the wrong question. He mentioned that although our motives were probably well intended, they were very misguided. Then he said something I will never forget.

He asked, "Why is the world looking to a rock star from Ireland to solve the problems in Africa, or to America to rescue us? The only one who can save Africa is the people of Africa."

The predictable and safe answer to our question would be one that patted us on the back for our concern, sharing some information about the various charities we could contribute to, and how we could pray as another way to help. But Dan turned it around and surprised us with an answer that was both unpredictable and controversial. We'd all heard the global conversation about America's role in helping to "save Africa," and this made Dan's response seem almost irreverent as it related to the world's view. But instead of being offended or repelled by his answer, you could sense every person on our team leaning in with heightened interest as to what he would say next. He went on to discuss the dynamics of African culture and its capacity to save itself. He elaborated on the urgent need for indigenous African leaders to emerge and create a better continent, a better nation, better cities, and better neighborhoods. He went on for a while longer, and we were all fully engaged; the content of what he said was incredibly interesting, and it resonated with us deeply. And just to be clear, Dan wasn't resisting foreign aid in Africa or anyone who leverages his or her influence to help. In fact he totally believes in partnerships like these; but he was defining what he believes will transform Africa in the long run.

As it relates to being interesting, I learned the necessity of being controversial when called for as I watched Dan in action. He reminded me of the boredom that comes with predictable, safe leadership, and the excitement that comes when there's controversy with substance. In this context, Dan's response met the question with the force and clarity it deserved. At the same time, he didn't leave respect, compassion, and grace behind. In addition, he earned credibility as our team saw firsthand the reputation he had developed throughout the African community, and the huge impact he was having there. Dan also spoke from a place of deep conviction, and his established credibility gave his convictions the strength of powerful influence. He didn't allow unnecessary obstacles like fearing failure or disappointing others' expectations to stop him from speaking up for his convictions and mission, which are utterly clear in his mind and heart.

There's something critical to point out here: motive is extremely important. He was not being controversial for the sake of being controversial. The motivation to be controversial is not about trying to be edgy or cool; it involves realizing when the moment calls for it, and having the courage to step forward with conviction. Dan didn't speak up to try to impress our team, and he wasn't just trying to be different for the sake of being different. Instead, he was saying what needed to be said to a group that was misinformed, and in many ways naïve. He recognized that our heart desires were sincerely motivated, and that we actually wanted to become aligned with his mission in ways we could help. He stepped into the moment with a posture of humility and an attitude of respect. Dan wasn't invasive, but he sensed he was going to meet us in our own desire to make a difference with a potential new insight and challenge.

Therefore, he saw this as an opportunity to bring clarity and intentional focus to our efforts, while at the same time changing our paradigm of how to invest in the people of Africa. Ultimately, he knew that what he was saying could have an exponential and positive effect on us, moving us to partnerships that aligned with this new way of thinking.

There is a difference between necessary and unnecessary controversy. Daring to be controversial in a mode that is relationally intelligent involves willingness to act or speak for the greater good of others, even if we need to relinquish our grip on harmony and personal comfort or put our fears aside. Relational intelligence involves knowing how to appropriately take advantage of the difficult moments, even if it makes others (and ourselves) uncomfortable. It involves fusing our own relational credibility with knowing how much to push people while not violating their trust. If we do this consistently over time, it will make us more interesting to be in relationship with because we'll become people who are willing to say the hard thing that others are unwilling to say. And if we dare to be controversial, others will show up in conversation expecting more than the mundane and obvious from us. People will develop anticipation for what we're going to say next. Being controversial should never emerge as an isolated reality; it is fused with credibility, strength of presence, and respect for the audience. That's the way of a relational genius.

When we as leaders do this well, the result is that those around us start getting interested in who we are and what we're about. When done right, it won't push people away but will pull them into our movement. As they find a window into our convictions, values, and mission, we'll encourage those looking to partner with people to change the world for the better. Instead of remaining predictable and mundane in our leadership, we must become more interesting by leaning into controversy when the moment calls for it.

Refuse to Be Irrelevant

There is a second way to become a compelling relator. Have you ever felt someone was talking *at you* rather than *to you*? He rambles on about something going on in his own life, or he talks about *his* interests, while remaining completely oblivious to *your* interests. Maybe you've had an employer give you a pep talk about how to get better at your job, but she remained totally unaware of the real issues your organization was facing. Subsequently, the conversation seemed disconnected from the reality of the situation. Or maybe you've been going through something emotionally difficult, and a friend is constantly complaining about some insignificant problem he's going through while you're suffering through deep emotional pain—it's maddening when she remains entirely unaware! In moments like these, people are not showing that they understand what is relevant to you and your life, and they miss the opportunity to relate to you effectively or be a positive influence on you—this is relationally unintelligent.

We all know how frustrating and boring it feels to be *talked at* by someone who lacks any relevance to us or our situation. It grates on us when people are oblivious and disinterested in what might be of interest to us, especially if they never ask or show they care. In this, many of us don't allow understanding of relevance to inform our own way of relating to others in leadership. More than we tend to think, leaders often forget to consider what's going on for the person on the other side of the conversation. They sometimes unconsciously assume that what is relevant to them will also be relevant to others, instead of taking time to consider what is relevant to the people around them. There's nothing we can do about other people's choice to remain irrelevant to us, but we do have

> There's nothing we can do about other people's choice to remain irrelevant to us, but we do have all the power to ensure our relevance to others.

all the power to ensure our relevance to others. Heightening our relevance in our relational spheres can guide us in becoming more compelling, and as a result, enhancing the quality of our relationships.

Remaining relevant happens in two spheres. First, it involves *cultural relevance*, which keeps us attuned to the concerns and contexts in the world around us. A second sphere comes through *interpersonal relevance*, which occurs through one-on-one conversation and helps us stay aware of the important issues people face every day. In either sphere, relevance revolves around listening well to others, discerning what is really going on in their lives, and then interacting with them so as to consider them and serve them well. To be fluent in both cultural and interpersonal relevance, we must seek to understand what people care about at the deepest level and learn how to meet them in that place.

Whatever opinion you have of Oprah Winfrey, one thing is for sure: she has mastered the refusal to be irrelevant, and it can be seen through the millions of viewers whose attention she captures. Her ability to stay relevant has helped give rise to her ever-increasing influence. She stays in touch with the culture and needs of ordinary Americans. She's relevant to their everyday interests and helps address people's desire to live better lives, whether it revolves around finances, health, careers, spirituality, or relationships. As she seeks to serve people well, being relevant has even led some to call her "America's pastor."

Whether or not you agree with Oprah's methods and philosophies, one reason for her success is her ability to be relevant to people's lives as they interact with the culture. To actualize our relational genius, we must emulate the same principle Oprah follows in how we lead, speak, and converse with others: *refuse to be irrelevant.*

Whether it's at work, in our church, or in the city we live, we need to speak and relate to people at this level. Whether dealing with our boss, a project manager, a team of volunteers, or simply a friend, if we learn to help others in ways that relate to what they're going through or what intrigues their curiosity, we will be more interesting to them, and consequently, more influential.

In the Scriptures, there's a scene I want to revisit from the life of Jesus where his journey intersects another woman's journey.[5] Jesus applied both cultural and interpersonal relevance to His interaction with her, and it reveals important aspects of becoming a relational genius. In a small Samaritan town known as Sychar, Jesus and His entourage of disciples stopped to rest at a historic well. It was about noon when Jesus found a spot to sit close to the well, while the disciples ventured off to find other provisions for the day. From Jesus' vantage point, He watched as a Samaritan woman approached to draw some water. In the culture of first-century Palestine, it would be highly irregular for a single Jewish man to speak with anyone possessing this Samaritan woman's profile of immoral reputation and questionable character (which was the reputation that preceded her and many people in her town and surrounding towns), not to mention the racial tensions that existed between Jews and Samaritans.

One reason this woman came to the well in the heat of the day was to avoid an interaction with any Jews. No Jews would ever be there at that time; they would surely come at sunset or sundown when it was cooler. In that culture, even if a Jew and Samaritan did cross paths there were clearly defined social, political, racial, and religious boundaries to keep Jews from talking to Samaritans, especially in a private setting like this, and especially if it was a Samaritan woman and a Jewish man. But as Jesus steps on the scene, His values and actions are different. He has come to the town of Sychar in Samaria tired from His journey, so He sits down by a well. When a Samaritan woman comes to draw water, Jesus strikes up a conversation.

Jesus: Would you draw water and give me a drink?

Woman: I cannot believe that you, a Jew, would associate with me, a Samaritan woman, much less ask me to give you a drink.

In that culture of the first century, a Jewish man with the appearance of a rabbi would never approach an immoral woman like this in public for fear of damaging his reputation. Because Jesus was a rabbi, He was breaking all kinds of invisible, but significant, cultural barriers with this confrontation. But Jesus was clearly intentional in doing this. The conversation continues.

Jesus: You don't know the gift of God or who is asking you for a drink of this water from Jacob's well. Because if you did, you would have asked him for something greater and he would have given you living water.

Woman: Sir, you sit by this deep well a thirsty man without a bucket in sight. Where does this living water come from? Do you believe you can draw water and share it with me? Are you claiming superiority to our father Jacob who labored long and hard to dig and maintain this well so that he could share clean water with his sons, grandchildren, and cattle?

Jesus: Drink this water, and your thirst is quenched only for a moment. You must return to this well again and again. I offer water that will become a wellspring within you that gives life throughout eternity. You will never be thirsty again.

Woman: Please, Sir, give me some of this water, so I'll never be thirsty and never again have to make the trip to this well.[6]

We notice that Jesus is tired and thirsty from His journey. He sits down to take a rest and asks the Samaritan woman for a drink. He begins a conversation by connecting to her initially in His humanity. After sitting down, He is physically exhausted, and most likely hoping to initiate a conversation with her, as He often does with others. His asking for a drink is a vulnerable request for her to help Him, thus revealing His human need. He probably hopes to build a bridge and give her a sense of dignity, while also trying to eliminate any tension that she feels in that moment as a Samaritan woman interacting with a Jewish rabbi.

Jesus actually chose to need people from the moment He was born throughout His life on Earth. When He relinquished his rights as God and became human, He was also giving up His rights to be entirely self-sufficient. Because of this, He was in touch with our same human experience. He knew what it felt like to struggle, to experience pain and loss, and to feel rejected by His close friends whom He loved so deeply. In fact, the Scriptures tell us not only that Jesus got tired and thirsty but, in other places, He got sad, angry, and fearful, and experienced emotional pain. At one point, He even felt abandoned by His Father.

In addition, the Scriptures tell us that He felt positive human emotions of joy and love, as well as what it was like to anticipate and hope. Jesus experienced ambition, and He knew the satisfaction of accomplishment. He entered the human experience in part so His humanity would connect to our humanity in a relevant way. He became one of us to relate to all of us. If we are to be relevant to people's lives, others need to see and know us in our humanity. They need to see that we struggle and have pain, as well as see our joys, ambitions, and hopes. They need to see that we have real physical, emotional, and spiritual needs. The truth is, sometimes we're irrelevant to others because in our own lives we're more like religious robots than real humans. At times, we act as though we're above elemental human needs, or at least exude that perception. Being in touch with our humanity helps us stay in touch with the human experience and know what others are going through, which can enhance our ability to be relevant to what they're going through.

In addition, Jesus also used a cultural reality to connect with the woman's life situation. He immediately found common ground and then used a relevant metaphor that connected to the longings of her heart. He contrasted the "well of water" with the "living water" that God Himself offers. A well was a big part of this woman's culture and daily routine, and that's why Jesus used relevant imagery to describe God in a way she could understand. He understood her world and what would make sense to her. This did not simply intrigue her; what He said connected her to her deepest longings, thus making Jesus more compelling to her.

Jesus connected a metaphor she was familiar with to the timeless reality of the thirst in her soul. He took a universal truth about human beings and individualized it to her situation, which helped her feel understood and known in that moment.

> Jesus connected a metaphor she was familiar with to the timeless reality of the thirst in her soul.

Jesus knew that to be human was to be thirsty, so He engaged her thirst in a unique and interesting way that intrigued the longing in her heart and made Him relevant. Though a well may not be the best metaphor to use in our context today in order to be relevant, the same principle of relevance applies. To be relevant, we need to use words and metaphors that remain salient to the current reality of people's lives.

I have a friend who was spiritually seeking but couldn't quite find what was true about who God was. She struggled with believing in God because of her family and spiritual background. She grew up in a Greek Orthodox Church that emphasized rigid rules, regulations, and traditions. It focused on the obligation to have everything always be in its right place, and this made her hesitant. In her mind, God wanted to put her in a cage where she would be unable to live freely or express herself because God would be angry if she broke a rule or tradition.

Because one of her great loves was being an artist, using art as a metaphor seemed to be relevant to her. In effort to describe God in a way she could understand, I told her one day that "He's less like a sheriff who tries to control and keep everything in its proper place, and more like an artist who uses humanity as His canvas to create beauty." I went on to describe how God wanted us to allow Him to shape our lives so He can create a beautiful masterpiece with us, where our truest human essence can be expressed, and so we can live most free.

If we're going to become more interesting in how we relate to others, and if we're going to intrigue them with our words as well as our actions, then we need to keep getting better at wrapping timeless, universal realities into individualized expression that meets people where they are. This is true relevance. This helps us connect with people in their humanity, and at times it helps other people in their search to find God. Being relevant to others doesn't happen by accident, but only when we make it happen.

Change the Way You Communicate

Though it is important to discover our own unique voice in how we communicate to others, there is something much more important to the communication process—*begin with the other person in mind*. Whether it's a conversation happening one-to-one (talking with one other person), or one-to-many (speaking to a group), this same communication principle applies.

> There is something much more important to the communication process than your unique voice: *begin with the other person in mind*.

My friend Allison is one of the most talented communicators I know. She's profoundly articulate, her depth is authentic and evident, and her presence is commanding and strong. Not long ago, she had an opportunity to speak at a church, and what she had to say was extremely important. However, the delivery of her talk hindered what she said.

It was her first time speaking in this community, and she began her talk with emotional intensity. She was confrontational in her approach, and what she shared made people feel uncomfortably guilty. After the talk, a couple of us discussed with her how she could have changed the way she communicated to help other people better receive what she said. We assured her that what she said was very important, but how she said it needed to change. Because it was her first time speaking in this context, a lot of people didn't know her, so naturally the emotional intensity seemed out of place, as if it were too much too soon. The confrontational approach didn't seem to be the best first step either, because the audience wondered why they were being confronted when they had just met Allison. At a motivational level, guilt was probably not the best strategy for long-term change.

But Allison's response to our advice was, "I can't change my style because I'm just going to say what God has put on my heart, and where it lands it lands. If it's a message God has put on my heart and it's true, then God will use it no matter how I say it." To some this may sound noble or filled with conviction, but the dilemma is that God, for reasons I don't fully understand, decided to use human beings to carry out His will on Earth. I don't think this means we relinquish our responsibility to consider how we're going to say what He's put in our hearts to say. In fact, I'm not aware of anywhere that God tells us that it doesn't make a difference how we communicate His life-changing message to humanity. I believe that He's given us the ability to use our words as bridges that build toward connecting to others, and ultimately connecting others to God. The Scriptures tell us in Acts 14:1 that Paul and Barnabas spoke so effectively that a great number of Jews and Gentiles believed.

Certainly God can use us even at our worst, but why wouldn't we strive to bring the best of ourselves forward? Why wouldn't we sharpen the dull edges of our communication skills to give our best efforts to honor God in the process? Truth is, Allison didn't think sharpening her edges would make her a stronger and more successful communicator. She didn't think *the how* mattered. Essentially, she violated the most important

RI principle when it comes to communication: *she didn't begin with the listener in mind.* And because she refused to change how she communicated, it's unfortunate that her impact suffered profoundly (she was less effective). Great communication is not choosing one or the other (that is, what or how), but a powerful combination of both. This principle is true when we're communicating one-to-one and one-to-many.

Effective communication is also a critical component to the leadership development process and has enormous implications for relational intelligence. As the director of a two-year leadership development program called the Protégé Program, I especially value communication in our emerging leadership process. Each year, our team interviews several dozen applicants from around the world to select twelve new protégés to go through our two-year experience. From the beginning, our team guides them toward becoming more interesting communicators because we believe not only in the mission and movement we're part of but in how effectively we must carry it out. On this journey, we strive to create opportunities for them to share the story of their lives with increasing effectiveness.

One example of how we help them develop their communication is by providing speaking opportunities. We invite them to give five-minute talks in front of a group of people, which is not as easy as it may seem. We invite a handful of seasoned communicators to carve out time to listen and offer insightful feedback through positive affirmation and critical analysis. Having just five minutes, they're forced to use their brief time wisely, and they quickly learn the importance of making every word count. This developmental environment challenges them to focus on talking about what's most important and most interesting.

In the feedback process, we zero in on improving both their delivery skills as well as the content of what they're saying (the how and the what). Through these experiences, we're able to coach them on changing how they communicate, while at the same time helping them discover their unique voice as communicators, which again plays out in one-to-one and one-to-many settings. Most important, we challenge them on "the why." In other words, listeners must be convinced why the topic matters for us to be most effective.

One foundational element that we emphasize with protégés is for them to stop assuming what most people assume in conversations: that people inherently want to listen. Too often speakers don't work hard to capture an audience's attention because they presume they have it. Just because someone shows up to a team meeting, an event, a one-on-one conversation, a class, or even a church, doesn't mean she or he inherently wants to listen to what we have to say, regardless of our position or status.

RI leaders understand these dynamics and work hard to convince their listener why what they have to say matters, and why they need to listen. The primary way they communicate this is by their approach to what comes across when they are speaking. Relational geniuses understand that people have a short attention span, not to mention that they are bombarded with an immense amount of information as they move through life. Relational geniuses know if their ideas are going to survive, they must work diligently and intentionally to capture people's attention. Every human being has the potential to become a more interesting person who has something to say, but so many fail in the pursuit to become effective communicators. Relational geniuses do whatever it takes to communicate with others most effectively because they know the result will be to have a significant impact and foster healthier relationships—even if this requires changing the way we communicate.

> Relational geniuses know if their ideas are going to survive, they must work diligently and intentionally to capture people's attention.

Activate Your Passion

One common denominator that I've observed with the most interesting people I know is this: *they have passion!* In fact, it almost doesn't matter what they're passionate about. Just being passionate about something makes someone more interesting. In contrast, passionless people are boring people. A failure to demonstrate passion is often why certain people aren't as effective in their field as others. When leaders lack passion, no one can tell that they care about what they're saying, even if they declare how important it is with their words. In whatever setting, whether you're a leader sharing your cause with a group of volunteers, a supervisor trying to envision your employees, or simply attempting to establish new friendships, one thing remains true: the more passionately you care about what you're saying, the more people will desire to listen to you, be around

> Passionless people are boring people.

you, and take part in your mission. More than anything else, your passion is what convinces people that what you're talking about matters—and people want to connect to something that matters.

My friend Ben is a brand new leader who serves as a volunteer at Mosaic. He's one of those guys who volunteers as much time as he can possibly give. He exudes passion in all his endeavors, which always ignites the passion of others around him. If we could clone his passion and reproduce it in others, we would.

One of the projects Ben co-leads is Project Homeless Connect. He's one of our representatives who helps us partner with other organizations to put on this annual event that seeks to serve the homeless community in Los Angeles. We gather hundreds of volunteers in numerous strategic locations all over the city to serve thousands in the homeless community in various ways. This past year, as Ben began the planning process, he started working with one particular humanitarian organization. He gave himself wholeheartedly to the planning process, as he does with everything. He was working one day with a man named Jimmy, who was part of this organization. Jimmy made a statement that surprised Ben but also brought clarity to who he would choose to lead in the future. He said, "Ben, you're very passionate about what you do, but I need to let you know that your passion will soon die out. Mine has, and I know yours will too."

To Ben, this was appalling.

When he told me this story, he was disturbed, and emphatically declared, "Jimmy is wrong! And I'm going to make sure he's wrong because I'm going to do everything I can to keep my passion red-hot. I believe what I'm doing matters, and I will always remember the importance of this cause. That guy was bored with his life and didn't have an urgent sense of how important our mission is, but I'm passionate about it, and that makes all the difference." (Can't you just feel his passion?)

> The more passionate you are about your mission, the more interesting you'll become in your leadership.

Ben is right. The more passionate you are about your mission, the more interesting you'll become in your leadership. We must refuse to allow our passion to die, because if it does it usually points to how bored we are with what we're doing. When you're bored with what you're doing, you will bore others.

One week later, the man who originally told Ben his passion would die saw Ben again. He pulled him aside to share something with him that once again surprised Ben. This time, he said, "What I told you last week was wrong. And since that day, I haven't stopped thinking about it. I left that interaction with you last week inspired to change because your passion was so remarkable to me. Ben, thank you for your inspiring passion."

When we lead with passion, it inspires others and pulls people into our movement. If you have difficulty leading with passion, maybe your mission is not big enough, or maybe you're just not carrying the urgency you need for your mission. It is no one else's responsibility to live and lead with passion— only yours. Leading with passion will prompt you to become a relational genius by helping you ignite passion in those around you through the relationships you establish with them.

When people aren't engaged in our vision, our movement, or our cause, it's easy to think that they lack the ability to remain interested, rather than *absorbing the responsibility ourselves* to become more interesting persons. If we struggle in our leadership to capture people's attention and engage their interests, we're not simply the victims who have fallen prey to the culture of boredom; instead we must allow this reality to motivate us to become more compelling relators. Relational intelligence requires us to resist the temptation to have a victim mind-set that blames others for not being interested in us or our movement. We must take responsibility to become the most interesting people we can be and to bring that part of us into our relationships. This will accelerate the path toward becoming a relational genius, and undoubtedly, a catalyst for our influence.

The Conversational Futurist

I skate where the puck is going, not where the
puck has been.

—*Hockey legend Wayne Gretzky*

Huse is one of my favorite TV shows, and even though Dr.
House is so mean, we fans can't help but love him. What
makes him stand above the rest in his medical profession
comes down to one thing: he doesn't merely diagnose; he prog-
nosticates. In other words, he sees where a disease is going and
gets ahead of it—not to mention that he's always right.

House isn't satisfied to face off with an illness as it presents
itself, as many of his colleagues are. Rather, he wants to outsmart
it, outrun it, beat it. This drive ultimately leads him to saving
patients' lives. It's almost as if he enters a time machine and
goes into the future to see the trajectory of the disease before
anyone else sees it.

The question is this: Is it possible to do the same thing when it comes to relating to one another through conversation? Can we step into a time machine and peek into the future awaiting us to help pull others to that future through the vehicle of our words? The answer is a resounding yes.

Like Dr. House, conversational futurists don't merely diagnose (understand the fundamentals of dialogue), they prognosticate (see where the conversation is heading). They know how to get ahead of where a dialogue is going and outrun it. Conversational futurists realize that every conversation is alive with potential and has the capacity to move forward and create change. They're driven to evolve a dialogue with intention and progress and are able to use their words as a medium to do so. As a result, they bring vibrancy and momentum to people through dialogue. They are the Dr. Houses of conversation.

Evolve the Conversation

Conversational futurists refuse to stall the dialogue or even circle around the same subjects simply by using different words. They shift gears out of neutral and increase their speed. They use speed not to accelerate the pace of their words but rather to enrich the depth and breadth those words bring. Conversational futurists see the power of evolution as it relates to dialogue and lead their conversations toward new dimensions of life and growth. When this happens, the person with whom the conversational futurist is talking experiences a new future where personal growth and progress are made. This becomes a portal of conversation that helps leave the past where it should be . . . behind.

Conversational futurists are seen in a variety of relational contexts, ranging from a leader dialoguing with a group, through one-on-one discussion with a friend or coworker, to a leader coaching another leader. One day, I was talking with Chris, a leader whom I respect. He asked me if there were any leadership challenges I was facing. I told him about someone on my team in whom I saw leadership potential. My challenge was that every time I tried to raise the bar for him to step up his leadership responsibilities, he would shrink back and his interest would fade. He did whatever tasks he was asked to do; he was faithful to the expectations of his role as a volunteer, and he was always diligent in his efforts to complete a project. However, he kept his efforts in the realm of tasks; where he shrank back was in leading people. Although I saw greater leadership capacity in him, I couldn't motivate him to take on increased responsibility as a spiritual leader with oversight of others.

My question for Chris was, "How do I help this young leader realize his potential and step into a role of spiritual leadership?" I was dwelling on the immediate problem rather than opening my eyes to the greater dilemma. In other words, I was circling around the same issue, causing the dialogue to stall. Chris, however, saw beyond what was right in front of him to where the conversation needed to go. In effect, he knew how to move our interaction with a high level of progress. Instead of suggesting a new way to challenge this leader to step up, he proceeded to address an entirely different issue from what I was asking. In fact, he didn't even answer my question. But he shed light on the true challenge that I wasn't able to see, thanks to my nearsightedness.

Chris said, "You are only looking at it from the perspective that he simply needs a little more motivation, but to me it sounds as if he's trying to tell you something else. By his refusal to broaden his leadership responsibilities, I suspect he's trying to tell you he only feels worthy to keep doing tasks. And if I were to guess, it's probably because of some personal struggles or character deficits that he needs to deal with first."

At first, the answer to my question seemed as if he had missed my point, but after a few moments of letting it sink in I realized that in fact I might be the one missing the point. In essence, Chris didn't give me a technique I was asking for in regard to motivating another leader or getting him to expand his leadership influence. Rather, he offered me the key to unlock the mystery behind why this potential leader was intentionally holding himself back. Many people in Chris's position would have suffered from nearsightedness, not seeing past the precise question presented to them and as a result stunting the life conversation.

What I learned from Chris's approach is to look beyond what's right in front of me, considering what isn't an obvious response but instead one that addresses a deeper issue than what's simply on the surface. It doesn't mean we always have the right answer, and it doesn't mean that we don't sometimes just address the question in front of us. However, this is how we can cultivate our ability to drive conversation forward and stay one step (or more) ahead. This involves seeing where the conversation needs to go in order to help the person we are interacting with move forward.

Every conversation has a life to it. Pulling it forward into the future is another way of saying that dialogue can evolve to its fullest potential. In other words, conversational futurists ensure that progress is made through use of their words. All of us can help make that reality happen in our relational circles, whether through friendship, leadership, or some other arena. But too often we find ourselves being what I call conversational backtrackers rather than conversational futurists. Instead of helping the dialogue evolve and move forward, we fall behind and find ourselves always trying to catch up in conversation. This hinders our ability to have an impact on others through our words.

> Every conversation has a life to it.

Think Before You Speak

One way to assess whether you fall behind in conversations is by asking, "What percentage of what I say in an ordinary conversation is formulated in my mind before I say it?" In other words, do you know what you're going to say before you say it? I asked a friend this question, and he told me that 90 percent of what comes out of his mouth is being simultaneously formulated as he's saying it out loud. When he begins talking, he doesn't necessarily know where he's going with his words or where he's going to land. He doesn't know where he wants to drive the conversation before he starts talking. Engaging in dialogue this way leads us to being a conversational backtracker because we allow the words that come out of our mouths to drift aimlessly. Consequently, substance of our conversation does the same. Our words lose meaning and fall flat because we are not driving them somewhere intentionally.

When we act as conversational backtrackers, we not only lose ground in bringing the conversation to its fullest potential, but we often retread the same ground that has already been covered. In essence, we digress rather than progress, and our opportunities to enliven our conversations suffer greatly. Allowing ourselves to drift into becoming conversational backtrackers is relationally unintelligent because we forfeit our role in bringing change and dynamic elements to our relationships through the potency of our words.

The obvious difficulty with falling behind is that it results in our being unable to lead. The dialogue ends up leading us; we're no longer leading it. If we're always following behind, we won't create movement through the words we say, and we lose our capacity to steer our conversations.

To become conversational futurists rather than conversational backtrackers, we must improve our ability to formulate our thoughts before we speak. Being more thoughtful and intentional in our speaking doesn't involve "filtering" our every word or being inauthentic as we relate to one another. Nor does it mean that we end up thinking so hard that our words sound scripted and flat. When we take the time to formulate our thoughts, we in fact create more honest, meaningful, and clear sentences that pave the way for further clarity and gravity in dialogue. As we think before we speak, we add elements of wisdom, provocation, and dynamic movement. The true challenge in doing this lies in our ability to remain fully engaged in what our partner in dialogue is saying, while at the same time engaging our inner thoughts to create a current of relevance and momentum in the words we are about to say. This ignites a spark that can impel the direction of our conversation forward.

> To become conversational futurists rather than conversational backtrackers, we must improve our ability to formulate our thoughts before we speak.

Assessing our thought process as we interact through dialogue can help reveal whether we're drifting in conversations without focused purpose, or whether we're being intentional with our words and know where we're driving our conversation. Gaining clarity here can open the door to becoming a conversational futurist rather than a conversational backtracker.

As leaders, many of us face obstacles in our effort to become conversational futurists and effect change in our relationships. We struggle to drive the dialogue in the way that brings life and evolution. It's not that we lack intellect or something substantial to contribute. Rather, most of us simply haven't practiced increasing our speed of thought, as well as our speed of articulating those thoughts in a way that furthers conversational momentum.

For those of us who struggle with conversational speed, we may wonder if it's even possible to become a conversational futurist. There's no doubt that all of us can learn to consistently get ahead of our dialogues and evolve them with intentionality. The primary solution comes down to practice, which means that no matter who you are, there is room to strengthen the conversational futurist within you.

One Ear to Heaven

As we begin to practice becoming a great conversationalist, we must remember to keep one critical thing in mind. The most significant way to get ahead of the conversation is to keep one ear to earth and one ear to heaven. By "one ear to earth," I mean listening to whom you're talking to and being engaged on a human-to-human level. And by "one ear to heaven," I mean listening to how and where God is guiding you. If we pay attention to God's voice, He can emphasize to us certain dynamics that could help a conversation move forward that we would be unable to discern on our own. This may include God highlighting to us certain words a person is saying that reflect the true nature of what the person is trying to communicate. This may be what we would need to know to move conversation forward. God may also reveal to us the momentum of a conversation that we aren't able to see without Him. No matter how good we are at advancing a conversation or bringing it life, God knows far more than we could ever know because He sees a future that we are unable to see.

If we're looking for ways to get ahead of the conversation and seek understanding of where the conversation needs to go, we can find the answer in listening to God as we open our hearts and ears to Him. So, as we travel through this chapter together and learn concrete ways to become conversational futurists, let's hold strongly to the mystical reality in which God works, through revelation and prayer. But now, let's explore a few of these ways that help us understand not only how to catch up but also how to get ahead of a conversation as we strive to pull the dialogue forward and bring life and growth to others.

New Yet Timeless Truths

On one occasion, a man named Nicodemus pursued a conversation with Jesus. He was a member of the Jewish ruling council, which was seventy respected leaders who had a high level of governmental authority (similar to the role of the Supreme Court). So, Jesus was dealing with a powerful, intelligent, and respected man. In addition, being a very devout Jew, he was skeptical about Jesus' teachings yet found himself intrigued by the power and grace Jesus demonstrated in His life.

As Nicodemus begins this dialogue, he acknowledges who he perceives Jesus to be: "Rabbi, we know that you are a teacher who has come from God. For no one could perform the signs you are doing if God were not with him." Although Nicodemus didn't begin this dialogue with a question, Jesus sensed strong curiosity within him. Seeing that Nicodemus was searching for the meaning behind Jesus' life helped Him get ahead of the conversation and pull it forward.

At first glance, Jesus' reply almost seems to overlook what Nicodemus has just said: "I tell you the truth, no one can see the kingdom of God without being reborn." This continues to intrigue Nicodemus. Jesus taps into his desire to understand the deeper dimensions of spirituality. We see his desire to understand as he continues the conversation: "How can anyone be born when they are old? Surely they cannot enter a second time into their mother's womb to be born!"

Jesus answers, "I tell you the truth, no one can enter the kingdom of God unless he is born of water and the Spirit. Flesh gives birth to flesh, but the Spirit gives birth to spirit. You should not be surprised at my saying, 'You must be born again.' The wind blows wherever it pleases. You hear its sound, but you cannot tell where it comes from or where it is going. So it is with everyone born of the Spirit."[1]

Nicodemus is captured by this conversation, and to express this he asks, "How can this be?" Jesus continues to evolve this conversation as great conversational futurists do. His next response is, "You are Israel's teacher, and do you not understand these things?" This is, of course, a rhetorical question, one that is more about Jesus seizing the moment to challenge Nicodemus on his understanding of what it means to be spiritual, that is, to be reborn with God through a life-changing encounter with Jesus. Although Nicodemus is deeply religious, until this moment he has not understood or fully grasped the path toward eternal life through Jesus. It is in this moment that Jesus is able to listen carefully, not necessarily to Nicodemus' exact words but to the curiosity behind them.

Jesus' approach to this dialogue is informed by paying careful attention to how Nicodemus is approaching it. In other words, He responds to cues from Nicodemus. Jesus seeks to gauge how much further Nicodemus wants to go in the conversation. He doesn't force His own agenda on him but instead recognizes what Nicodemus is longing for, and then steps into the conversation with a posture to serve Nicodemus' best interest and bring life not only to the conversation but to Nicodemus himself.

Once Jesus realizes that Nicodemus is opening himself up to Him, He presses into the moment and begins to guide him into a deeper, spiritual dimension. He recognizes his spiritual curiosity and moves him toward understanding how he can have a life-changing encounter with God.

In essence, Jesus is describing a timeless truth in a new way that connects to Nicodemus' deepest longings. It is a "new truth" for Nicodemus to realize that not only did he have a human birth but he also needs to have a spiritual birth. Though this has been true for all eternity, this is a new truth to Nicodemus. This is an example of Jesus outrunning the conversation and getting ahead of where it is going. Instead of discussing something that is already known or understood, we too can introduce something that's not known by a person on a conscious level but that deeply resonates at a soul level. Jesus could have simply reaffirmed what Nicodemus said by discussing the power of God, which is the topic that Nicodemus began the conversation with. But instead, Jesus got ahead of the conversation and introduced a new, yet timeless, truth to him that ultimately transformed his life and perspective.

Just like Nicodemus, sometimes people who are searching for God, people who are trying to meet their deepest longings, are wrapped in power, status, wealth, or intellect. Sometimes they even appear spiritual or religious, as if they have it all together and don't have questions, doubts, and fears. But the truth is, there are people all around us who disguise their soul searching and who are looking for someone to guide them into the deeper dimensions of life. They don't always tell us directly what they long for, which is why we must listen carefully to what they're really saying. Unfortunately, our lack of relational intelligence—primarily our inability to listen better and our tendency to force our agenda on them—often stifles other people's pursuit of deeper conversations with us. If we listen better and with more attentiveness and respect, we can begin pulling people forward in conversation that resonates with their soul. It is possible to know where another person wants to go in a conversation and come alongside to guide her toward her heart's longings—just as Jesus did with Nicodemus.

To become conversational futurists, we must learn to listen to the questions people are asking even if they aren't being spoken in question form. Sometimes people make comments because they're testing us to see whether we want to engage the deeper questions they have. They're often seeing if we can be trusted to go to that vulnerable place with them of their own human neediness. Our dilemma is that we often don't notice what they're really trying to say, or we hear them and (because we don't give careful thought to what they said) we take the easy path of just reaffirming their thoughts, feelings, or perspective, rather than driving the conversation forward with wise and loving intention.

> To become conversational futurists, we must learn to listen to the questions people are asking even if they aren't being spoken in question form.

Forward Progress

Maybe you're like me, and you sometimes find yourself in a conversation that doesn't feel as though you're contributing anything new. Even if you're engaged in the conversation, you find yourself just affirming what ought not be affirmed simply to make someone feel good, or restating the obvious in a different way, neither of which helps the conversation evolve. But in many cases, by not pulling a conversation forward we end up pushing people backwards.

I have a friend named Kelly who continuously pulls forward whatever conversation she's in. On one occasion, Kelly and her friend Emily were discussing Emily's recent break-up with her boyfriend. Emily was expressing her inability to forgive her ex-boyfriend because of how badly he treated her, and how he had misled her about how deeply committed he was to her. In that situation, many of us would probably have sensed her frustration and pain and most likely affirmed her feelings to help her cope or vent. We may even have circled the same point over and over again in various ways, in the name of being a good friend. In doing this, we might think we were meeting her perceived emotional needs, but this is an example of contributing to a static, momentum-lacking dialogue. We get stuck in the present because we are unwilling, or maybe unable, to move the conversation forward.

But not Kelly; she happens to be a believer in bringing every dialogue she's in to the farthest point possible. In doing so, both she and the people she interacts with experience an evolution of sorts, thus fueling faster growth and allowing greater awareness to occur. In this conversation with Emily, Kelly in a sense was able to pull herself into the future of where the dialogue needed to go, and she chose to help lead it there. She did this by asking intentional questions: "Why do you think you have such a difficult time forgiving him? Have you ever hurt or betrayed anyone in your life that required someone else's forgiveness?

Looking back, can you think of any times where you recognized him violating your trust and you decided to look past it instead of confronting him?"

At first, Emily was a little perplexed and even offended at some of these questions because they were not driving the conversation in the way she wanted at that moment. But knowing that Kelly always had her best interests at heart, Emily decided to remain open and follow her lead. Kelly listened to Emily's thoughtful responses and acknowledged her pain. In appropriate time and with sensitivity and love, Kelly then pulled the conversation forward with her words. She shared how Emily would never be able to forgive her ex-boyfriend until she deeply realized her own need for forgiveness. This is ultimately where Kelly perceived that the conversation needed to go. Kelly sensed that Emily not taking any personal responsibility and therefore could tell that she was going to continue to drown in her own hurt, anger, bitterness, and resentment. This wasn't merely good insight but a positive force of dialogue that breathed growth and life into the moment. In one sense, Kelly outran Emily's attempts to keep the dialogue stagnant and brought dynamism that got the conversation where it needed to go. In the end, it advanced their friendship and propelled Emily out of bitterness and into a healthy view of what had happened. This freed her to deal with her pain, but also move forward.

Conversational futurists resist the temptation to simply reaffirm what a person wants to hear. They maintain the courage and wisdom to press into any unhealthy thinking patterns. If they identify something like a person taking no personal responsibility, they are willing to address it with sensitivity, love, and truth. Furthermore, because Kelly knew that Emily valued forgiveness, she could use that to help her guide the conversation toward where Emily really wanted it to go. It wasn't a forced conversation or domineering agenda; it was more like a dance where they moved together in a way that bred relational health.

Interpreting the Signs

Another way to become a conversational futurist is through interpreting the signs of what's going on around you. When we interact with people, we can see signs pointing toward where they're heading, and if we learn to help them connect the present with the future, then we can become better conversational futurists. Sometimes the signs are extremely obvious, but we don't notice because we're not looking in the right place. If we want to get ahead of a conversation, we have to learn to make the connection between cause and effect in someone's life. Seeing the relationship between cause and effect is like stepping into a time machine and transporting into another person's future. We see the trajectory of where their choices are taking them before they even get there. As we help others see these signs, we develop the ability to move people forward by offering them a perspective on their future.

> If we want to get ahead of a conversation, we have to learn to make the connection between cause and effect in someone's life.

Jesus addresses this dynamic of interpreting the signs and identifying the connection between cause and effect. On one occasion as He's trying to empower people to change the way they are living, He becomes frustrated because people are not paying attention to what's right in front of them. Jesus uses a metaphor to articulate his point: "When evening comes, you say, 'It will be fair weather, for the sky is red,' and in the morning, 'Today it will be stormy, for the sky is red and overcast.' You know how to interpret the appearance of the sky, but you cannot interpret the signs of the times."[2]

Jesus is dealing with the principle that there's evidence of what is to come if we just look for it. Simply put, if we see that the sky is gray and overcast, we know it's going to rain. There is evidence all around us about where people's lives are going, and there are many scenarios where this can be seen. Maybe you know someone in whom you see signs of apathy and can tell his life is going nowhere. Maybe you know someone who's ignoring advice from everyone around her and you can tell she's going to crash and burn. On the flip side, maybe you know an emerging leader who has been serving with faithfulness and diligence, and you can tell the person is on the brink of something great. Or maybe you know a young leader who is gaining confidence in the ability to lead, and you can just tell this person is going to be a strong force of good in the world.

Sometimes seeing cause and effect in people's lives plays out in the negative and other times in the positive. Then there are those other times when you could simply be showing people that the presence of God is all around them, and you just help them notice it in their lives. Whether someone is apathetic, living a destructive lifestyle, lacks integrity, is on the road to greatness, or is on the verge of becoming a positive force in the world, what people choose consistently reveals the life they are creating for themselves. Conversational futurists have developed the ability to see and interpret the signs, as they help people connect the dots of cause and effect in their lives.

I have tried to cultivate this skill of seeing the connection between cause and effect so I can better bring progress to my conversations, whatever the context. For example, in a series of talks with my friend Brad, it was almost impossible to miss the signs that were flashing from his life. Although Brad is a highly talented, charismatic, and intelligent guy, he was going down a very destructive path. I witnessed him telling white lies to people for no apparent reason other than to make himself look good. I saw how he looked at girls when they weren't looking, and it was not in the respectful way they deserved. I saw his arrogance growing stronger as he grew more successful in his life. Finally, I saw him slowly slipping away from his relationship with God as he talked less and less of his gratitude and more and more of his disappointment in God and his sense of entitlement.

The signs were obvious to me, but at the same time, they would have been easy to overlook not only for others but even for Brad himself. Brad was well liked and trusted by those around him. At the time, he was in a committed relationship with an amazing woman, whom he was going to ask to marry him. His arrogance was often masked in an aura of confidence. He still attended church regularly, and he even wanted more leadership responsibility. Serving on one of my teams, he asked one day if he could speak at a weekend gathering. But I was concerned for my friend because I saw a clear view of where his future was heading. The lies and deception would catch up to him and he would break trust with those he cared about most. I knew that his overarching low view of women would begin to poison his relationship with his girlfriend. I knew that his arrogance fueled an overinflated view of himself, thus opening the door for moral failures of all kinds that he was unprepared for owing to his pride. Most important, I could see that his devotion to the God he said he loved so much was slowly withering away into nonexistence.

Just as Jesus referred to our ability to look around us and see what was coming, I was able to look at Brad's life and see the texture of his future. I chose to discuss some of these matters with him along the way, sharing with him about where I believed his life was heading. I did this because I valued and loved him as a friend. As we talked about the evidence his life was showing, and how these signs were pointing to a certain and destructive future, he began realizing things he hadn't thought about or even seen in his own life. He was shocked at how he had allowed his bad choices to thrive in his life. He had not been able to see clearly where the signs in his own life were pointing. Through our conversations, his eyes were opened to the storm brewing around him. In essence, he saw the red and overcast sky as behavior he was creating, and he even began to see his future unfolding before it happened. The good news is that he took action to change his life course in the present because he could now see the life he was carving for the future.

There are times when we know, humbly speaking, that we are right in our assessment of the trajectory of the life of someone we know and care about. Seeing the signs in someone's life isn't just about identifying unhealthy or destructive patterns, and it's not simply about finding error in someone's ways. We must also remember that it isn't judgmental to be honest about where we see someone else's life heading because of the destructive choices they are making. Interpreting the signs to help someone change course is one pathway in which a conversational futurist brings the other person to life.

> Interpreting the signs to help someone change course is one pathway in which a conversational futurist brings the other person to life.

Relational intelligence involves people talking about what they see in another so as to honor and respect the other person. They offer advice, but the reality we must embrace is that people may never see it as we see it, or change the choices they're making because of what we've shared with them. No one is always able to pull people forward to produce results, and this is why the journey requires us, at times, to release the results of our efforts to God. The results should never be the sole reason we do or don't engage these meaningful and sometimes difficult conversations. In fact, our motivation to pull people forward is best expressed when our primary desire is to serve someone's best interest and bring the person to life.

If it makes you feel any better, realize that Jesus didn't always get the results He hoped for either, even though His motives were pure. When He engaged a conversation with the rich young ruler as recorded in the Gospel of Luke, He essentially told him that his wealth would end up owning him, and that if he wanted to experience eternal life he would need to let go of his clenched, white-knuckle grip on his wealth. Unfortunately, that day the rich young ruler decided to continue making choices that would erode his personhood, those that continued to stand between him and God.

Sometimes our impact happens through one moment in a conversation, and other times it's about a series of conversations in a friendship or relationship where you talk about the signs and patterns you see along the way. To become a conversational futurist doesn't require a certain amount of life experience, extraordinary intelligence, or personality type. It simply starts by helping people connect the dots of cause and effect in their lives. It will require courage to share our honest thoughts in a loving way with people whose path we cross. Maybe as much as anything we must remember that being a conversational futurist is all about serving people's best interest with humility, honor, and respect, especially if we're challenging them to change.

Reversing the Assumptions

One final way to become a conversational futurist is to reverse the wrong assumptions of a conversation. Underlying assumptions are often the cause of static dialogue. They foster predictable, mundane, and non-thought-provoking conversation, thus not allowing the person to evolve into fullest potential. When we let the wrong assumptions drive a conversation, we put our mind in neutral and therefore are reactive rather than proactive. But if we address wrong assumptions that people make, artfully and meaningfully, we can immediately change the momentum of a conversation. Our mind moves out of neutral and we shift from gear to gear as we drive it forward.

In one leadership context I was in, I observed a conversational futurist as he interacted in a question-and-answer session. He reversed the momentum of an underlying assumption, thus changing the direction of the conversation. Instead of falling behind, he got ahead. In that specific context, the group was discussing the importance of focusing its energy on improving strengths rather than expending energy trying to fix weaknesses. The conversation was alive as people experienced self-discovery about their own strengths and talents. After thirty minutes of discussion, one woman in the crowd asked the speaker, "Don't you think it's better to live out of our weaknesses because the Scriptures say that God is made perfect out of our weakness, rather than focus on our strengths?"

Although she asked this in the form of a question, the speaker realized this was more of a statement in question form and was also wrapped in a wrong assumption. The underlying assumption was that Christians who live out of their weaknesses honor God more than when they focus on their strengths. If the speaker had allowed this assumption to determine the momentum of the conversation, his response might have driven people to take less responsibility to develop and use their strengths to serve God and others, thus allowing themselves to be identified more in their weaknesses. This approach would also have caused the conversation to regress. In essence, it would have left them thinking that this was God's preferred way to honor Him with their lives. So he had to address the hidden assumption in order to redirect the conversation. What he chose to do in that moment held elevated importance because his response was going to be the framework that most people in the room remembered.

What he said was this: "As human beings, even in our greatest strength we are incredibly weak, so why should we start from a greater deficit when God is the one who has given us our strengths to begin with?" He went on to elaborate, and his response immediately changed the tone of the room. He did so without attacking his questioner. He embodied what it meant to be a conversational futurist.

Mistaken Assumptions

We can see the powerful effect of this principle in the Scriptures as we read how Jesus interacted with people. On one occasion, people gather around Jesus to listen to Him teach. Some religious people bring a woman to Him who was caught in an adulterous relationship. They make her stand before the group. In effort to trap Jesus and establish a basis for accusing him for letting her off the hook, they say to Him: "Teacher, this woman was caught in the act of adultery. The Law of Moses commands us to stone such women. Now what do you say?"[3]

Jesus bends down and starts to write on the ground with His finger. They keep on questioning Him, and He straightens up and says to them, "If any one of you is without sin, let him be the first to throw a stone at her." Again He stoops down and writes on the ground. At this, those who hear begin to go away one at a time, the older ones first, until only Jesus is left with the woman still standing there. Jesus straightens up and asks her, "Woman, where are they? Has no one condemned you?"

"No one, sir," she says.

"Then neither do I condemn you," Jesus declares. "Go now and leave your life of sin."

We don't know exactly what Jesus wrote on the ground with His finger, but in this moment we do see Jesus shift the entire momentum of the conversation. This religious crew has an agenda to disgrace the woman, as well as catch Jesus in the act of breaking a law in public. That's where the momentum is going. But Jesus doesn't surrender to it. Instead, He reverses the underlying assumptions that the religious people are making. They presume to know how Jesus will respond, but obviously they are wrong. They also assume that they are better than, or even holier than, the woman who has committed adultery. They may be thinking judgmentally, "How could anyone be so immoral?"

Jesus doesn't avoid the truth or sidestep the question. He is getting ahead of what is happening right in front of Him so He can help bring life to this moment. He doesn't allow a misinformed, even judgmental assumption to dictate His response. In other words, Jesus takes back control of the conversation instead of allowing Himself to be trapped by a hidden assumption. Jesus attacks the assumption that her sin is worse than theirs, that certain sins are more deserving of punishment than others. In essence, when Jesus reframes the conversation and communicates to them that they too have missed the mark of perfection, the momentum changes.

> Jesus takes back control of the conversation instead of allowing Himself to be trapped by a hidden assumption.

Jesus could debate them about whether they should stone her or not, which is how many Christians choose to engage moments like these. But He makes a point that everyone standing there has sinned, and that all of them are equally deserving of punishment. At the same time, He chooses a kind, compassionate, and gracious way to make His point, yet without relinquishing honesty and truth. In what seems to be an intense moment when everyone waits to hear how Jesus will respond, He remains sensitive and compassionate to the person who is furthest away from God. Unfortunately, Christians usually do the opposite. They end up polarizing the person in the room who's furthest from God rather than seeking how to draw the person closer.

We can, like Jesus, learn to assess where the group is trying to take the conversation. Conversational futurists develop the ability to gauge where someone on the other side of the conversation is driving the momentum of the dialogue. Then they have to decide if this is where they want it to go, or if there is a hidden assumption that they need to address or redirect, which would entail their attempting to shift the conversation a different direction.

The Future Is Waiting for You

When conversational futurists focus on seeing past the present and into the potential evolution of dialogue, they face the great possibility of outrunning the lifeless strand of words that are fighting to set the tone of countless conversations. By pulling dialogues forward with intention, they cultivate healthier relationships and bring people in their spheres of influence to life through conversation—the most elemental way of relating to one another. If we look at ourselves as the Dr. House of conversation, and learn to emulate his drive, we can develop an ability to outsmart and outrun our dialogues. And like Dr. House, we'll get ahead instead of falling behind, lead rather than follow, and ultimately create change rather than leaving interactions the same as when we began them. If we implement the key actions from this chapter, we will find ourselves a little bit smarter when it comes to relational intelligence.

The Likeable Hero

Being likeable requires work.
—*Tim Sanders, The Likeability Factor*

When it comes to making great films, screenwriters constantly hear from studio executives, "How can the hero in the story be more likeable to the audience?" It's because they know how critical likeability is to successful filmmaking. The best filmmakers strive to evoke favorable feelings in their audience for the hero of their story, and if they fail they know the impact of their film will suffer. The less the audience likes the hero, the less captivated they will be with the unfolding plot. The most successful filmmakers grasp this important concept so much that if they don't make their hero likeable, they know they'll lose a large portion of their audience—not to mention it'll cost them lots of cash.

This same principle transfers directly to relationally intelligent leadership. If leaders don't embrace the importance of likeability, they'll lose a significant portion of their audience, and their relational impact will suffer. Every leader represents a story that is unfolding, one others will either be captivated by or become quickly disinterested in. Consequently, leaders have the potential to become heroes to those around them if they learn to capitalize on being likeable. But if they don't, their influence will be diminished, and it will cost them greatly.

Likeability 101

Likeability is a fundamental characteristic of relational intelligence, and we tend to underestimate its effect in our leadership endeavors and everyday lives. Contrary to what some people think, likeability is not about trying to become a professional people-pleaser, or trying to be all things to all people. What makes likeable people relationally intelligent is revealed in a person's ability to evoke favorable feelings in their "audience" (that is, the person they're in a relationship with), in order to produce a positive outcome that serves others well. Whether people are leading a team at work, at a party with friends, or living their ordinary day-to-day lives, what likeable people do best is establish authentic connections with people that make others feel valued and cared about.

> Likeability is a fundamental characteristic of relational intelligence, and we tend to underestimate its effect in our leadership endeavors and everyday lives.

Likeable people are enjoyable to be around. They seek to find common ground where there is division, create laughter and levity where there is tension, and emulate a sense of well-being where there is discontentment. Truly likeable people are relational geniuses because they embody certain characteristics that evoke favorable feelings in others. They realize the critical nature of likeability to accelerating their leadership impact.

Any Objections?

Some may be skeptical about elevating the importance of likeability. One objection might be that it ought not be emphasized because the mission is far more important than the likeability of a leader. In one sense this is true. But this objection is valid only if likeability is prioritized over the mission itself. If likeability is seen in its proportionate value, it will enhance the quality and speed with which your mission gets accomplished. When likeability is in its proper place, it doesn't undermine or diminish the mission but strengthens it instead.

The connection between carrying out our mission and practicing likeability can be compared to the human body. Let's say the skeleton represents our mission. It is the structure that holds all the working parts together. Essentially, it's the core framework from which the physical body functions; thus it is irreplaceable, and of central importance. And let's say the skin covering the skeleton, which is warm to the touch and appealing in appearance, represents likeability. The skin does not take away from the necessity, functionality, or value of the skeleton but instead covers the internal hard structure with warmth. So when you touch the human body, what you feel is life and warmth, while the core structure maintains its integrity and strength. In essence, likeability is the flesh that wraps itself around the skeleton—that is, the mission.

> If likeability is seen in its proportionate value, it will enhance the quality and speed with which your mission gets accomplished.

Likeability causes our core framework (the mission) to be inviting and warm, and why shouldn't it be that way? In fact, it's practically as essential as the skeleton is to the human body. If you want to carry out your mission with likeability, you must ponder how others experience your leadership. Do you evoke feelings of life and warmth through how you lead that serves others well? Do people feel the warmth and life of who you are through the way you interact with them? Or do people experience your leadership as solid, but also as a hard, rigid, cold structure?

RI leaders don't lead with all skeleton and no skin, but neither do they lead with all skin and no skeleton. If either were the case, it would be all presentation and no substance, or all substance and no presentation. To be sure, carrying out your mission won't be optimized if it doesn't encompass both skin and skeleton. RI leaders see the important relationship between mission and likeability.

There are other possible objections one may have about embracing the value of likeability. To some, it may seem like a polished or glamorized version of manipulation, or even feel patronizing when implemented in leadership contexts. It could seem like the equivalent of being a "schmoozer." But this objection is substantiated only if likeability is used as a tool to further one's own self-driven agenda, and failing to authentically care for those who are helping to carry it out. True likeability is not just a path to whatever end you're seeking for yourself, or merely a means to an end. Rather it is more like one of the legs you use to walk down a path toward your goal, synergistically working with other virtues and values of relational intelligence to serve other people well. When functioning correctly, likeability is all about serving others and adding enjoyment to a moment or relationship.

One other objection is that likeability may seem unnecessary to achieve success. To be sure, there have been many people who were successful in leadership without being likeable. Although it's not always needed to reach some level of success, I believe it is needed to achieve your greatest level of success.

All of these objections are worth considering, but ultimately they should not inhibit us from embracing the value of likeability because it is absolutely essential if we want to reach our full potential and become a relational genius with powerful influence. If nothing else convinces us, it can't hurt us to become more likeable, while our leadership can certainly suffer if we relinquish the importance of it.

The Genius of Likeable Heroes

In the realm of leadership, our primary dilemma to pursuing growth in likeability is that we often don't have an accurate gauge of how liked or unliked we really are. Therefore, we tend not to know where we need improvement. To discover the hidden power of our relational genius, we must begin by honestly assessing how likeable we are so we can identify the path toward personal growth in this arena of RI. In an effort to explore how we can become likeable heroes, let's look at five signs to guide our quest.

FIVE SIGNS OF LIKEABILITY

1. Approachability	Likeable people are relationally inviting, accessible, and approachable.
2. Stickiness	Likeable people maintain consistent, long-standing, loyal relationships.
3. Rapid trust formation	Likeable people create relational space for rapid trust to be formed.
4. Friendliness	Likeable people exude relational warmth and kindness, and actively pursue people.
5. Flexible optimism	Likeable people embody a high yet realistic level of optimism about work, life, and relationships.

Are You a Likeable Hero?

Sign One: Approachability

Likeable people are relationally inviting, accessible, and approachable.

Approachable people are easy to meet, talk with, and get to know. They have an inviting spirit in how they interact with others, constantly opening themselves up to the people in their lives. They communicate to others that they have relational entry points, meaning they make themselves accessible to others by maintaining an enthusiastic posture about meeting new people, and allowing those they already know to get to know them even more. They choose to establish an authentic connection with others by expressing an openness of spirit toward them.

In contrast, unapproachable people close their relational entry points; they usually communicate a lack of openness to meeting new people and are often closed off to wanting to get to know those with whom they're already in relationship. They communicate to others that they are too busy or too important for them. When you interact with someone who is unapproachable, he is often aloof and distant, with little expressed desire to get to know you (nor does he allow you to get to know him). His posture and body language remains closed off. We sometimes recognize them as people who never smile or exude relational warmth. People can sense when we have an open or closed door in our life. The question we must ask ourselves as it relates to approachability is, do we invite others into our relational space through a posture of approachability, or do we send the message that we're closed off to them?

I was recently inspired by the powerful impact of one CEO's posture of approachability as it relates to building a business and establishing a company culture. In 1998, twenty-four-year-old business mogul Tony Hsieh sold his company, LinkExchange, to Microsoft for $265 million. A year later, he began a different kind of company, selling shoes on the Internet: Zappos.com. They have more than sixteen hundred employees, and last year they had more than $1 billion in sales. But this company's path to success happened differently from what most would expect.

CEO and cofounder Hsieh decided he would not focus his company on selling shoes to make the most profit; rather, his brand would be to give the best customer experience on the planet. Tony reports that his true passion isn't shoes specifically but instead customer service, no matter what he's selling. He displays tremendous relational intelligence as he understands the irreplaceable link between true success and relating to people well, both within his business as a whole and also specifically as the CEO. He as well as his company emulate a very approachable ethos in many ways, primarily through their customer service.

As a business, Zappos strives to create the best possible customer service experience. They've observed what makes people feel devalued and frustrated in the purchasing process when dealing with businesses, and to ensure customers have the best experience they've created a number of policies:

- When someone calls Zappos, she gets connected to what they refer to as their Customer Loyalty Center, where every customer speaks to an actual human being every time; there's no outsourcing to other countries.
- There are no impersonal scripts given to employees on how to dialogue with customers about common issues that arise.
- Sales aren't commission-based.
- Employees aren't restricted with a time limit on a customer phone call.
- If a customer calls looking for a specific shoe that is out of stock, or if she can't find her size, Zappos employees research the three best competitors' prices and suggest those Web sites.

In essence, Zappos makes it extremely inviting and easy for a customer to choose them as a place to spend hard-earned money. So what does customer service have to do with being approachable? Many people don't want to choose a company where there are unnecessary obstacles to overcome, thus making them unapproachable, inaccessible, and uninviting. They don't want to go through automated voice systems, or customer care reps who can't speak their language fluently. They don't want to subject themselves to memorized scripts when they need more individualized help, or feel pressured to spend more than they intended when they're already making a purchase. And they don't want to feel cutoff while on the phone thanks to time restrictions, or deal with someone who cares more about profit than helping them.

Hsieh figured out that there is a strong connection between success and approachability. When it's only about the bottom line, it just becomes about what someone wants to take from people, rather than maintaining the best posture toward the customer. This is true not only in our relationships that encompass our business endeavors but also in our personal relationships. Ultimately, if we don't remain approachable and inviting, we lose out on our level of impact, and a part of our soul gets compromised as well. In essence, Hsieh wants the soul of his company to be warm and inviting. And this has paid off.

> Hsieh figured out that there is a strong connection between success and approachability.

The Zappos customer base is extremely loyal (75 percent of sales are repeat customers) and they have an extremely low employee turnover rate. In fact, after the first week of training, in order to weed out employees who don't resonate with company values, Zappos offers every new employee $2,000 to walk away from the job. Amazingly, only 10 percent take the offer. Zappos also furnishes their employees free food during work hours at their onsite cafeteria, snack machines that are available to all employees but don't require money, and 100 percent payment of all employee health benefits. These are just a few of the things Zappos does to communicate an inviting spirit in their company culture, among employees and customers. Employees like the company so much that they remain loyal and choose to pass up "free money" in order to work at Zappos. Customers like the company so much that they keep coming back over and over again. Zappos knows that *being likeable matters*.

As a businessperson, Tony Hsieh raises the value of approachability, and as the CEO he also shows this sign of likeability. One powerful way he embodies this can be seen through something I've never heard of any CEO doing. Instead of having a big corner office with a beautiful view like most executives, he has chosen to sit in an ordinary cubicle with everyone else in the middle of the office. This is wholly intentional on his part, to show his employees that he is approachable. He also receives an annual salary of only $36,000 in an effort to communicate in a profound way that he's not "above them."

Zappos is an all-access company, and Tony is an all-access leader. He embodies an open-door mentality that the entire company has embraced as part of its culture. This relentless posture of approachability is an example to us as we translate this RI principle into our everyday relational lives and leadership endeavors. Likeable people make it easy for others to relate to them by remaining approachable, accessible, and easy to be around.

More often than not, CEOs or employers such as Tony, are seen more as villains than heroes. They can be overpowering, domineering, and almost entirely unapproachable, therefore making the people who work for them always feel like the underdog. But Tony takes a heroic stance as he chooses to embody likeability as a virtue, and raises the underdog up to his same status, placing himself on equal ground with the rest. He empowers rather than overpowers, emulates humility rather than arrogance, and welcomes others into his relational sphere rather than pushing them away. Like a hero, he doesn't just rescue the underdog but envisions the underdog as part of his mission.

What would happen if we took this "sit in the middle of the office" approach while carrying out our leadership endeavors? What would happen if we made ourselves more accessible to those around us, no matter what level of leadership we are at? What if we became more inviting with the people in our lives and removed the unnecessary obstacles to make it easier for people to interact with us? If we carried out this value in our relationships, our approachability would increase our likeability, which would catalyze our efforts for greater impact.

It will increase your impact because, just like Tony, people will start rooting for your cause and your mission, be drawn to work with you, and be compelled by your valuing of people. In addition, their desire to follow you will increase, and ultimately their belief in you will expand exponentially. They'll want to emulate both who you are and how you are, because after all, who doesn't want to be a hero?

I've personally experienced the power of approachability in hiring people, and when I'm deciding to volunteer on someone else's team. The more approachable someone is, the more apt I am to hire them, and the more likely I am to want to serve on their team. In addition, if people are approachable, I'm more apt to be friends with them, promote them, and partner with them in a cause. As a leader, the more approachable people are, the more opportunities I want to give them, and it even makes me more open to mentoring them.

Being approachable not only increases our impact but also enhances the quality of our personal life because the more room we open up in our hearts to allow people in, the fuller our lives will be. Our relationships grow stronger. People we meet immediately feel included and valued. Instead of cumbersome obstacles to overcome, there's an invitation extended to them to be part of our life. And for that, we become likeable heroes. Whether in our careers, volunteer activities, personal life, or some other arena, relating to people in this way is a true sign of likeability.

Sign Two: Stickiness

Likeable people maintain consistent, long-standing, loyal relationships.

In simple form, someone who is "sticky" is someone others want to be around, and that results in creating loyalty and low turnover in whatever context you're in. For example, when it comes to the workplace, one survey shows that 46 percent of people quit their job because of a poor relationship with their supervisor.[1] In *Three Signs of Miserable Job,* Patrick Lencioni states that two-and-a-half million people quit their job every year; the number one reason for quitting is that the employee does not want to be around his or her manager.[2] These statistics point to a lack of stickiness among managers and supervisors.

In contrast, sometimes people keep their job not because they like the job itself but because they like their boss despite the job. Whether at work or in other social contexts, likeable people have a sticky effect on others and consequently create long-lasting and loyal relationships.

One way to determine if you are a sticky person is to ask yourself, "How much turnover do I experience in my relationships with staff, friends, and other people in my life?" If a lot of your relationships are short-lived, this usually reveals that they are unsticky. If this is true about you, whether at work or in your personal life, there are probably reasons related to your lack of stickiness that point to a deficit in likeability.

It may sound obvious, but people prefer to work with people they like. Employers tend to hire people they like. Supervisors are more apt to promote whom they like. Consumers tend to buy from those they like. Even at a party, people want to drink a beer with people they like. I know this can be a frustrating reality for some in their work environment because they're certain that competence, intelligence, and tenure are more important than likeability, but we must not underestimate the influential power of establishing strong relational connections, which leads to stickiness.

In fact, where you may lack abilities that you wish you possessed, likeability is able to cover the gaps. Specifically, being sticky will ensure loyalty and enthusiasm around your cause or mission. This is also true in the superhero world.

In a poll to determine the most beloved superheroes of all time, the rather predictable number one choice was Superman, chosen primarily for his abilities. But what I found most fascinating was the selection of the number two superhero and the reason for his popularity. This second most beloved superhero is Spider-Man.

According to About.com: Comic Books (http://comic-books.about.com), what Spider-Man lacks in ability, he makes up for in heart. The wall-crawler is one of the first of many true-to-life superheroes, and because of this, Spider-Man is beloved and adored by fans all over the world. What it comes down to is that even though he may not have the greatest and most alluring powers, he does have heart and is extremely likeable. And that's why he is in no want of loyal fans.

> Being sticky not only magnifies your heroic abilities but also helps close the gaps where you fall short.

You may never be Superman, but you do have heroic potential. And being likeable will help others have the eyes to see it. Being sticky not only magnifies your heroic abilities but also helps close the gaps where you fall short. Then others will stick around long enough to see who you are and what you are truly capable of, thus creating a loyal and committed following.

This dynamic may be revealed in someone who runs a company or nonprofit organization with long-standing employees. We may also notice it on a volunteer team where people stay on the team for a long period of time. It's not always that they just have a passion to serve in that particular arena, although they certainly might. Rather, it's often because they like the team leader, and as a result they've stuck with him or her. Even when someone's passion to serve that specific group of people fades, the loyalty created through stickiness will strengthen the person's staying power over time.

Of course, long-term is relative if you're a young leader, but paying attention to who stays on your team, or how frequently people leave or quit the team, can give you a glimpse into your own stickiness. Pay attention to when people are loyal to the relationship you have with them because it usually reveals a high level of stickiness—a true sign of likeability. One of the best signs of stickiness is when others actively pursue spending time with a leader. Matt is a friend of mine who quite often has people join his team, which serves and mentors high school students. People who don't even have a strong desire to be around teenagers end up volunteering to serve, mentor, and invest in their lives, simply because they like being around Matt.

In some ways, it appears that Matt cultivates stickiness by accident, but it's actually an intentional form of RI that he's developed. If Matt weren't likeable, he wouldn't have as many volunteers to mentor high school students, which of course would negatively affect his breadth of influence. He knows that the more adult volunteers he has, the more time each individual teenager can receive mentoring. To him, this heightens the importance of likeability in his leadership. In other situations, I've seen people whose biggest passion is mentoring teenagers, so they join a mentoring team. However, once they realize that they don't like being around the leader of the team (thanks to the leader's unlikeability), their passion to invest in teens dissolves. As a leader, if you ever suspect that people avoid you, or you notice a pattern of people wanting to leave your team within a few months—or even if you find it quite rare for anyone to actively pursue spending time with you—these may be signs of unstickiness revealing a lack of likeability. If we're not careful, sometimes we can become relationally repellent without even realizing it, meaning that people stop wanting to be around us.

To be sure, if we are unpleasant or irritating to be around, we won't be sticky. If we are consistently insensitive, or even cruel; if we talk too much or remain overly self-centered in conversation, people will not want to be around us. The same is true if we're disingenuous or just plain arrogant. The great danger here is that leaders often remain unaware of these unlikeable interpersonal dynamics in themselves. If you wonder why people don't seek you out as much as you'd like, why they don't have a passion to be on your teams, or why you have a hard time recruiting and keeping volunteers or employees, consider that you may lack a high level of stickiness. If you're willing to be honest about this, your journey can move you to identify and change certain behaviors so that you become a stickier and more likeable hero to others.

Sign Three: Rapid Trust Formation

Likeable people create relational space for rapid trust to be formed.

A relational genius knows how to use likeability as a key to establishing trust. Likeability alone doesn't ensure trust, but it does open up the possibility wider for trust to develop. When it exists, likeability creates relational space that can accelerate the speed in which trust is formed. One guiding principle of RI is this: *the more likeable you are as a leader, the faster people trust you.*

> Likeability alone doesn't ensure trust, but it does open up the possibility wider for trust to develop.

Have you ever met someone you liked immediately, and within a few minutes you found yourself trusting what she or he was saying? Maybe it wasn't necessarily for a reason based on pure logic, but you just sensed trust being established quickly. It wasn't noble character, brilliant intellect, or extraordinary competence that earned it; trust simply happened because of the way she or he interacted with you. They were likeable.

When I was in college, I decided to start going to church. I remember walking in for the first time, and Marty spotted me. When he greeted me, the first thing I noticed was that he seemed genuine and caring. He immediately began asking questions about me with sincere and curious interest. Right away, I could tell he valued me as a person and cared about who I was. I was impressed. The next time I saw him, I took a risk and asked him if he would mentor me. Essentially, I was declaring that I trusted him. It was not because of a long-standing reputation, or a relationship we built over time. It was not based on his brilliant intellect, and not even his leadership competence. At this point, I decided to trust him simply because I liked him.

This is a unique kind of trust. It is not the same as the deep and intimate trust between a husband and wife who have spent years establishing it. However, this kind of trust does have powerful implications. First impressions matter more than we give them credit for. In an ordinary moment of greeting and interacting with people, we never know what a relationship might turn into. A relational genius lives with the heightened importance of knowing that people have instinctive reactions that can either establish or hinder whether they'll trust her. She realizes that first impressions can cause a person to choose to be part of our movement, or choose not to be.

As Marty mentored me month after month, I was pulled into the movement and mission he was part of. Along the way, his impact shaped my personal convictions, leadership philosophy, and spiritual growth process. His influence on my life helped inform some of the major decisions in my life, some of which would change its entire trajectory. His mission and philosophy fueled in me a new way of living that shaped my future, and later it affected the future of others in a positive way.

If I fast-forward the story, I can say he has become one of my life mentors, a hero to me, and his impact has left a profound legacy in my life. It all began with rapid trust formation that happened in the relational space of his life and mine. That's the power of where likeable first impressions can take us. In an effort to become a leader who can accelerate and expand other people's ability to trust, Marty revealed to me the profound importance of how likeability can create wider possibilities for trust to be formed. The more likeable we are, the faster people will trust us, consequently accelerating and expanding our influence.

Sign Four: Friendliness

Likeable people exude relational warmth and kindness, and actively pursue people.

On Sunday nights, our Mosaic community gathers at a nightclub in downtown Los Angeles. Every week, new people attend from all walks of life and spiritual backgrounds. Because there are hundreds of people at the club every week, it's sometimes hard to know who's new and who's not. Because of this, we maintain a high level of intentionality about finding new people because we want them to feel welcomed and valued as individuals, no matter what their background or life story. One way we do this is by building a team of volunteers who we call socialites. Their entire job on Sunday nights is to be friendly. They roam around the club as social headhunters who are trying to find and meet all the new people.

These social headhunters always have time and space to make new friends. Their life is never too full to add more people to it. These are the women and men who actively pursue others and who can quickly establish authentic relational connections. They're the friendliest people we can find, and friendliness is often what makes people feel they matter. They contribute to creating an ethos that welcomes new people with warmth and intentionality. These socialites recognize, and live out, the value of friendliness, and as a result become heroes to others.

To increase our friendliness doesn't mean we have to be extraverted or charismatic, or even have an outgoing personality. It's not about how many people you interact with, whether you like social events with lots of people, or dinners with a small number of them. Friendliness describes how you choose to interact with others, no matter what the setting or what your personality type. This is about exuding warmth with people—and not just with new people, but with everyone you interact with. If you want to become a relational genius, you must do what social head hunters do: be friendly. And if you do, you'll become a hero to many who stand on the outside looking in.

> Friendliness describes how you choose to interact with others, no matter what the setting or what your personality type.

Sign Five: Flexible Optimism

Likeable people embody a high yet realistic level of optimism about work, life, and relationships.

Martin E. Seligman is a scholar in psychology who has devoted decades of his life studying optimism; he is also the former president of the American Psychological Association. Not long ago, Seligman coined the term *flexible optimism* to describe people who maintain wisdom in assessing situations through identifying when a pessimistic inquisition is required, and when a moment demands optimism. He offers insight into the advantages of pessimism to help achieve clarity when critical decisions need to be made about things that could negatively affect a person's career, family, leadership, relationship, finances, and so on. In addition, he suggests the dangerous side of optimism.

Though optimism by itself carries many positive benefits, it also has limits. For optimism to fuel likeability, it must move from blind optimism to flexible optimism. Relational intelligence doesn't require us to dismiss pessimism in our relationships as if it doesn't have a place; it's simply ensuring that we put it in the right place. Seligman argues that pessimism can bring perspective in vital choices that we make in our relational world because it can offer us a strong dose of reality amid unpredictability. It takes into account the dynamics of cause and effect. Pessimism can help us consider the potential negative results of our choices and actions, which can often have positive results in our relational world.

For instance, let's say a young couple starts dating and begins to fall in love, but the entire scope of their relationship has been filled with problem after problem. Their optimism says, "Problems are part of any relationship; it will all work out." But a good dose of pessimism helps them consider that their problems could be reasons to refrain from getting married quickly, or maybe at all.

Seligman says, "The bigger the consequences if things go wrong, the more you should apply the reality check of flexible optimism." The goal for a relational genius is optimism with eyes open, moving from blind optimism to flexible optimism. We must be able to use pessimism's keen sense of reality when we need it, without having to dwell in its shadows of darkness.

Flexible optimism increases likeability, while blind optimism and perpetual pessimism can lead to a lack thereof. The reason is that over time, others lose respect for leaders who see a false reality (who are overly optimistic) or who approach leadership challenges with naïveté, or overinflated idealism. People also lose respect for leaders who have a constancy of negativity and cynicism in how they see and interact with the world around them. Leaders who are out of touch with reality, in overly positive or overly negative ways, have more of a tendency to be disliked because people want to follow leaders with a healthy dose of realism fused with the fullness of optimism. Knowing and applying this is what makes flexible optimists relational geniuses.

Flexible optimists have an appeal to others who are surrounded by a culture full of negativity and cynicism. They're able to lift those who are discouraged or disheartened by how they see and experience the world around them. They do this through their positive but realistic outlook on life, work, and relationships, which can lift people who are drowning or in despair. Flexible optimists are likeable because they have the ability to shift people's perspective about life's circumstances, strengthen others to move forward when life doesn't go their way, and even dissolve the negative emotions of bitterness, cynicism, and resentment. Over time, this is how their optimism expands their ability to gain a voice of influence in people's lives. Their realistic but hope-filled outlook becomes a contagious positive virus that infects others and enhances the well-being of the people around them.

What the Signs Tell Us

These signs tell us how likeable we are. All of us have the capacity, potential, and ability to continue down the path toward becoming a relational genius by choosing to increase our likeability. As you assess yourself, these signs can point to your level of likeability and guide you toward personal growth in this arena. As you were reading through these signs, maybe there were one or two that stood out to you most as areas of needed improvement. Or maybe there were three or four of them you need to work on. If you can't find any of them to improve, I'm certain a friend, coworker, or family member can help point out a few of your less-than-likeable tendencies. However you choose to assess your own level of likeability, if you want to grow you must be willing to be honest with yourself and identify what your blind spots might be. Then you must tenaciously and intentionally pursue change. If you continue to develop the art of likeability, it will expand opportunities for your influence and enhance the quality of your relational world.

The Spider-Man Way

Likeability can get us further than we think. And what we lack in abilities, we can, like Spider-Man, make up for with heart. Every one of us can become a likeable hero in our own story, and along the way, we'll find loyal friends, devoted team members, and supportive people who serve alongside us in our mission.

The Disproportionate Investor

Disproportionate investors have disproportionate influence.

—*Cheri Hill*

Modern-day geniuses such as Wendy Kopp think of ways to do things that no one has thought of before. She not only imagined a new way of doing something, but through her commitment to invest in people who invest in others, she was able to make her dream become a reality. Relationally intelligent leaders see the connection among success, influence, and investing their time and relational energy wisely. Now, Wendy's new vision is being actualized, in large part, thanks to her ability to invest well. She saw enormous problems that couldn't be solved in a small way. Instead she knew that they would require her to be resourceful and strategic in building relationships with certain types of people.

As a senior at Princeton University, this twenty-one-year-old woman couldn't understand why college students weren't being as aggressively recruited to work in education as they were to work at corporations, especially considering the importance of education. She wanted to help solve this problem, which she sees as one of the greatest challenges in America today: children across the nation aren't receiving an excellent education. So she embarked on improving public education in America. From her vision and investment in this calling, she built a nonprofit organization from the ground up called Teach For America. This NPO works to offer a quality education to children nationwide, thus helping to solve the education crisis, what she calls "the greatest social injustice in America."

Wendy knew that tackling this problem was a massive undertaking, especially because she was only one person with a limited amount of resources to accomplish it. Her brilliance was seen in how she developed a plan to strategically recruit the nation's most promising future leaders, rather than simply taking anyone she could get. She knew the only way to ensure the building of a quality organization would be to select highly qualified people. Not only did they have to be qualified but they also had to be passionate investors in children. Wendy decided to recruit top-tier college graduates and called them to commit two years to teach in the most impoverished, under resourced urban and rural public schools in the country. No alluring salary was offered, but instead the potential to have a life-changing impact in the lives of kids who desperately need a better education. One example that reveals her compelling success is seen at the Ivy League's elite Yale University, where 10 percent of all graduates now apply to Teach For America.

On completion of their two-year commitment, these teachers are likely to assume positions of influence, some in education but the vast majority actually going into other sectors such as business, medicine, engineering, or law. But this is what Wendy wants because she believes these two years will change people so much that their lives will be devoted to making this vision to change public education in America a reality, no matter what field they pursue. She says, "What you learn through this is so transformational that you'll never leave behind what you learn. You'll be part of a group of civic leaders who affect fundamental changes in society. We need CEOs who understand these issues. We need doctors who understand these issues. We need policy makers who understand these issues."[1]

> Wendy Kopp believes these two years of teaching will change people so much that their lives will be devoted to making this vision to change public education in America a reality, no matter what field they pursue.

Teach For America continues to channel the best young leaders they can find against one of the country's greatest social injustices—and that requires leadership. They don't just look for teachers but leaders who want to give themselves sacrificially to making a difference in the lives of children. Wendy thinks carefully and strategically about who and where her NPO will invest its time and energy. They recruit people who they believe will have the most impact on the future of education, people with extraordinary talent, and perhaps most of all they look for leaders who want to give themselves selflessly to others in a way that brings about justice and change.

One of the challenges we face in our relationships is that people tend to be consumers, not just of products and services but of other people. To combat this within her organization, Wendy fearlessly asks for young people to sacrifice and give beyond themselves. She stands in front of groups of people, casts her vision, and asks, "Why wouldn't you do this?" The people who step forward are not the consumers, but those with the

> The spirit of investment is revealed most in the spirit of sacrifice.

strongest desire to give their lives away in sacrifice and service to others. Wendy understands that the spirit of investment is revealed most in the spirit of sacrifice. This can be compared to what Jesus called his followers to do when He said: "For whoever wants to save his life will lose it, but whoever loses his life for my sake will save it."[2]

Teach For America is relentless about who they select because they want every ounce of their investment in every teacher's life to have an exponential impact in the lives of children nationwide, and in public education as a whole. Wendy is what I call a disproportionate investor because she embraces the importance of investing in the right people. As a result, her influence grows with a disproportionate effect.

When it comes to our leadership endeavors, embracing this same level of engagement involves careful and strategic thinking about whom we invest in. Just like Wendy, every one of us has a limited relational capacity, so if we want to avoid having our best efforts wasted by those we invest in, we must elevate our intentionality, and invest wisely and strategically. If we do this, we too will become disproportionate investors, and along the way we'll keep increasing our relational intelligence. Our investment in a few of the right people will evolve into influencing many.

Purses with Holes

People are relationally unintelligent, even foolish, when they don't choose how to spend their time in a discerning manner. They fail to consider the future implications of their choice of whom they invest in, and they end up wasting their time on consumers who take, rather than spending their time on investors who give. Just think about it like this. None of us would willingly throw money into a hole if we knew it would be wasted. So why are we sometimes willing to spend our investment on people who have holes in them, knowing that our investment will probably be wasted?

The ancient prophet Haggai talks about this idea of how some resources are wasted thanks to the greed inside people: "Give careful thought to your ways. You have planted much, but have harvested little. You eat, but never have enough. You drink, but never have your fill. You put on clothes, but are not warm. You earn wages, only to put them in a purse with holes in it."[3] The prophet reminds us here that our everyday needs—planting, eating, drinking, putting on clothes, earning wages—are important, but we must not allow the pursuit of them to be an excuse to be consumers. What the prophet Haggai knows is this: if we're absorbed with taking for ourselves, we'll never feel as though we have enough. The misconception about consumerism is that no matter how much you consume for yourself you'll never be fully satisfied.

If we wonder why our relationships don't have more exponential impact, if we struggle with getting the people we're investing in to invest in others, maybe we've been spending time with people whom Haggai describes as "purses with holes in them." Have you ever found yourself investing in people who seem to have holes in them? You invest so much, but it never seems to make much difference. Maybe you find yourself spending quality time with someone in an effort to help the person grow. Could it be that you do this through some form of mentoring, coaching, or just personal dialogue, but the person never changes? Or maybe you've even invited the person into your home, to join your team, or given him or her unique developmental opportunities, but no matter what you do, your investment keeps leaking out of the holes in them.

Consumers Versus Investors

If we want a return on our relational investment instead of it being poured into a purse with holes, then we must learn to identify the difference between a consumer and an investor. This aspect of relational intelligence can guide us toward becoming more strategic in where and how we spend our relational energy.

Consumers always look for what they can take from others, while investors always look for what they can give to others. Instead of trying to hold onto something that's been given to them, investors give it away. In other words, they multiply someone's investment in them. Investors always focus on how they can make a contribution in their relational world, and how they can reproduce more good in someone's life.

> Consumers always look for what they can take from others, while investors always look for what they can give to others.

Consumers are relationally greedy and never satisfied with the investment someone makes in them. No matter how much people give themselves to a consumer, it's never enough. It could be someone you're mentoring who remains constantly ungrateful for every hour you spend with him, all the while demanding more time. It could be someone in your small group or on one of your volunteer teams who always seems to dominate the conversation and turn it to herself. She doesn't even seem to have the capacity to be interested in other people, much less make a positive contribution in how she gives herself to others. No matter how much investment a consumer is given, he always feels that he deserves more and becomes angry if someone doesn't give more.

Not long ago, I began mentoring Jeff. I met with him once or twice a month over a one-year period of time. During our times together, I would ask him questions and listen attentively to what he was going through. If he seemed discouraged, I offered encouragement and affirmation. If things were going well and he achieved something he was proud of, I would celebrate his life, hard work, and success.

I thought I was offering a valuable and positive investment in his life—until one day when he asked me for input on his strategic plan at work. I first shared with him about the numerous strengths of his strategy, and then I shared one thought that I didn't think would work that well. I simply offered him my honest opinion because he asked, and I'll never forget his response as we sat in the front seat of my car. He turned on me sharply.

After more than a year of investing in him, within seconds after discovering our disagreement, he was bitterly angry toward me. He began yelling, telling me all the ways I was wrong, how much I had failed and disappointed him, and that he had never trusted me or felt affirmed by me. As you can imagine, I was taken back, even stunned. I realized his emotions had probably been brewing over time, and that it was his moment to explode on me.

As I looked in the rearview mirror of our relationship I realized that there were clear signs I shouldn't have been investing significant time mentoring him, mostly because of his consumerist mentality. He lacked gratitude, seen in how he never seemed to get enough from me. We'd spend two hours together, and he'd complain that I didn't give him adequate time and attention. He was always absorbed with his own agenda, which I thought was selfish because he never maintained interest in anything or anyone else. Also, I noticed that he didn't spend time investing in others, nor was his heart positioned and willing to serve others. I invested in him mostly because I believed (falsely) that he needed it more than others.

Though at times it appeared he wanted to learn from me, he had all the signs of a consumer who takes all he can get. I would constantly try to guide him toward change in his life but always walk away feeling drained of my emotional energy. For various reasons, I chose to overlook his consumer qualities, until it finally backfired on me.

Basically, in that moment in the car I realized the entire year of investing in him would show no return. He would not take any of what he learned from me and share it with others; it was all for his own good. This was a hard lesson learned about the behavior of consumers, but one I'll never forget. His human value was not the issue; rather, I wasn't going to be the one to invest significant amounts of time in him because of what I now knew was the end result. He was a purse with a hole in it. If the people you are investing in are not giving their lives to invest in others, if they are self-absorbed, if they are ungrateful or even unteachable, then chances are they're consumers, and your investment in them may have no return.

Consumers always seek unhealthy forms of self-fulfillment through their relationships. They devour every ounce of relational and emotional energy for themselves, draining it right out of you. A true sign of this happening to you is felt when you interact with someone who always seems to drain you because she always wants something more from you. At best, she sees the cup half empty and wonders where the other half is that she deserves from you. She maintains a demanding spirit and is never satisfied. In other words, instead of seeing your investment in her as a gift, she is focused on how you have failed or disappointed her, and she wonders why you're withholding more from her.

A sure sign of an investor is seen in the people who energize you practically every time you interact with them. They enter relationships looking to give more than they get and to make a positive contribution even if it's just a brief moment. Investors realize that what they have to give to others is not dependent on what has been given to them. Instead, it comes from what they are willing to give. No matter how little or much we've been given, if we choose to serve others generously and willingly we'll be more fulfilled in our relational world. Investors actually know what it's like to be unexplainably full because they give generously of themselves to others and always remain open-handed with what they have to offer people. At the same time, they

> Investors realize that what they have to give to others is not dependent on what has been given to them.

are wise in who they invest in, seeking to minimize any leadership investment that might be deposited into a purse with a hole in it.

Going Underground

Although there are people in whom our investment gets consumed, or even wasted, there are also people in whom our investment gets multiplied. The truth of this reality is seen precisely in this parable:

> It's also like a man going off on an extended trip. He called his servants together and delegated responsibilities. To one he gave five thousand dollars, to another two thousand, to a third one thousand, depending on their abilities. Then he left. Right off, the first servant went to work and doubled his master's investment. The second did the same. But the man with the single thousand dug a hole and carefully buried his master's money.

> After a long absence, the master of those three servants came back and settled up with them. The one given five thousand dollars showed him how he had doubled his investment. His master commended him: "Good work! You did your job well. From now on, be my partner."

> The servant with the two thousand showed how he also had doubled his master's investment. His master commended him: "Good work! You did your job well. From now on, be my partner."

> The servant given one thousand said, "Master, I know you have high standards and hate careless ways, that you demand the best and make no allowances for error. I was afraid I might disappoint you, so I found a good hiding place and secured your money. Here it is, safe and sound down to the last cent."

The master was furious. "That's a terrible way to live! It's criminal to live cautiously like that! If you knew I was after the best, why did you do less than the least? The least you could have done would have been to invest the sum with the bankers, where at least I would have gotten a little interest.

"Take the thousand and give it to the one who risked the most. And get rid of this play-it-safe who won't go out on a limb. Throw him out into utter darkness."[4]

The master distributes his resources, not equally or fairly but as he chooses. Then he entrusts each servant with those resources, not telling them precisely how to manage them, or even what to do specifically with what's been given to them. Each person is positioned to succeed, but the third servant decides to dig a hole in the ground and cling tightly to what he was given by hiding it from anyone else. He played it safe, revealing only a selfish desire that caused him not to risk anything, which produced nothing in return. The other two servants chose to invest the resources they were given, and both of them multiplied the investment entrusted to them and received praise from the master who gave it. What we do with what we've been given matters. When the servant who had buried what was entrusted to him came back to the master, he was confronted and admonished. In one biblical translation, the master says to him, "You wicked, lazy servant!" We see how furious the master is at what this servant chose to do with this investment in him.

At Mosaic, our lead pastor, Erwin McManus, has an approach to investing in his paid staff that has taught me a lot about wise investments. One of his values in hiring new staff is not to hire anyone from outside of our faith community, for two main reasons. First, it keeps our team focused on developing leaders from within our community. Second, it allows us to truly know the depth of a person's character who is being hired before the person joins our team. No one has ever been hired at Mosaic before first being a volunteer, including our lead pastor himself. There is one remarkable quality that he identified with all of our paid staff team way before he hired them: that we would be generous and sacrificial investors of other people. It drives our lead team and fuels how we carry out our mission. As a result of this investor's spirit, instead of burying what's been entrusted to them, they double and triple whatever has been invested in them. That's what it means to be a disproportionate investor.

I remember when Erwin was asked by another leader, "How do you manage your staff and ensure they work the right amount of hours?" Erwin's response was, "I don't have to manage my staff because I hire people who I trust are fully on board with our mission. No matter how much I manage them, I'm certain they will give of themselves with full devotion, and even sacrifice, because they are compelled to give their lives away to serve others." When choosing people you will invest in, choose investors who give themselves generously for the sake of others because they will create exponential impact out of anything you invest in them. Then you don't have to worry about what they're trying to take from you, or what energy they want to suck out of you. In fact, they'll give more to other people than you could ever even ask them to give.

The core essence of an investor revolves around their stance toward people, and even their stance toward God. Investors see themselves as stewards of what God has given them, remembering that every relationship is an undeserved gift from God. They even see opportunities to invest in others as an honor and privilege from God. Their instinct is to be contributors in every relationship of their life. They are poised to love others through serving them, and even willing to sacrifice if necessary. Investors choose to be grateful about what they've been given and seek to generously multiply what they give to others. While the consumer encompasses a demanding spirit, a mentality of "I deserve whatever I get" and "You owe me more," the investor has discovered a secret joy found only in giving life away to others. They believe the words of Jesus: "It is more blessed to give than to receive." If we want to become more relationally intelligent, we must minimize our investment in consumers and maximize our investment in investors. Then our impact will become disproportionate compared to our direct investment.

A Few Good Men

Jesus saw the critical importance of how and whom we invest in with absolute clarity. He didn't try to change the world through politics, or with money; not by human power, or even through charisma. He forever changed the world by investing relationally in twelve broken and fragmented human beings, well known as His disciples. He saw potential in them beyond what anyone else could see at first glance.

> If we want to become more relationally intelligent, we must minimize our investment in consumers and maximize our investment in investors.

On one occasion, my curiosity was sparked as I pondered how much time Jesus actually spent with these disciples. So, I decided to read the four Gospels in the New Testament with one specific lens: How often was Jesus with His disciples? What I discovered surprised me. Whether He was performing a miracle, walking from one town to another, involved in conflict with religious people, or teaching to a crowd, in almost every single chapter He was with them. I consistently saw phrases such as, "as Jesus and His disciples were traveling through town" or "Jesus turned to His disciples and said . . ." Again and again, I observed the value Jesus showed for spending a great deal of time investing in His disciples, who were also investors.

While Jesus lived on Earth, He chose to spend a disproportionate amount of time with a few good men, who would have been viewed as misfits among their peers and the surrounding culture. I sometimes wonder about the accusations He faced on account of His investment choices. Sometimes this happens to us. It wasn't that Jesus only invested in His disciples, but also in people He encountered in passing moments. For example, He healed the blind man's eyes as He wiped mud on his face, and He spent time talking with Zaccheus, who He noticed climbing a tree just to see and hear His teachings. Jesus certainly spent strategic time with certain people, but in some instances, He actually passed over people choosing specifically not to invest in them.. For example, Jesus healed only one person among many who were waiting to be healed at the Pool of Bethesda. Why didn't He heal all of them? Although I don't know all the reasons Jesus chose to spend time investing in some and not in others, why He healed some and not others, I do know that just because He chose not to invest a certain amount of time and energy in someone, didn't mean He devalued him or her as an individual. Relationally intelligent people cultivate the ability to make these distinctions in their everyday choices.

Maybe you've been accused of not valuing someone because you don't spend enough time with him or her, or maybe you've been accused of being unfair with your time. Jesus, who was God in flesh, knew He'd have to make decisions to favor His time with some people and not with others. It wasn't because He valued them more as human beings; rather it was more likely because He thought strategically and intentionally about how best to carry out His mission on Earth. Truth is, there were so many people that Jesus wasn't able to interact with, much less invest significant time in. And within those human limits, He had to focus on maximizing His efforts so He would receive a return on His investment, and exponentially multiply His influence even after He left Earth. The more we minimize our investment in takers, the freer we will be to maximize our investment in givers.

> The more we minimize our investment in takers, the freer we will be to maximize our investment in givers.

There are exceptions to the principle of investing in investors, and we can see them in passing moments where Jesus healed someone but not everyone. He didn't necessarily know every single person He encountered, which means He didn't know if they were investors when He invested in them. However, in moments throughout his life He still chose to invest in them. More than anything, it was because He desired to do the Father's will. For us, if God calls us to invest in someone who doesn't look or act like the person we think will maximize our investment, of course this is the spiritual trump card over any leadership strategy of our own. I'm not declaring an absolute rule that allows us to ignore certain kinds of people, or not reach out to the outsider, stranger, or deeply broken person. I'm not suggesting that we can dispose of any human being, no matter who. But I am offering a guide for us in how to use the majority of our time the best we can to do the greatest good in the world for the greatest number of people. This is the example that Jesus gave us.

> Relationally intelligent leaders minimize potentially wasted investments and maximize potentially greatest investments without devaluing anyone in the process.

God desires us to pray fervently and think wisely, carefully, and strategically in where we expend our best leadership efforts. Relationally intelligent leaders minimize potentially wasted investments and maximize potentially greatest investments without devaluing anyone in the process. After all, this is what Jesus did with His disciples.

The Gravity of Selection

To select His disciples, Jesus began with fervent prayer, hoping the Father would guide Him with wisdom. He knew that in the near future He'd be delegating leadership responsibility for building the New Testament church primarily to these men. There was enormous gravity to His selection process, as

He wisely, prayerfully, and strategically chose His Twelve. His approach was not to take just anyone who signed up; He was extremely intentional in whom He chose. Then, after selecting His men, He began carving out significant time teaching them, inspiring them, confronting them, encouraging them, nurturing them, rebuking them, and challenging them to live and carry out God's mission. Not that long afterward, Jesus began entrusting them with profoundly important leadership responsibilities. His strategy of prayerfulness, selection, investment, and entrustment worked. It's through Jesus' strategy that He started a world-changing, history-shaping movement that's been going on for more than two thousand years. If Jesus' plan worked, then why don't we pay more attention to emulating His strategy? There had to be specific characteristics about His disciples that caused Jesus to choose them and invest in them so extensively, thus becoming a disproportionate investor. Haven't you ever wondered what informed His selection process?

Making Your Selections

As the director of the Protégé Program, a two-year leadership development experience for emerging leaders, I have the responsibility for choosing twelve new protégés every year. I sift through dozens of applicants with the interview team, talking with each one initially over the phone. Then, three to five people on our team (including me) interview them in person when they come to Los Angeles. Afterward, we collaborate and share our thoughts, observations, and analysis, and then I prayerfully select the twelve. As the interview process unfolds, characteristics of each potential protégé emerge, and we do our best to select the women and men who will be a good fit for our program. At the top of the list of what we look for are people who embody an investor spirit. I also happen to think this was one of the requirements Jesus posed in selecting His disciples.

A few years ago, when I launched the Protégé Program, I knew it would be an enormous devotion of time and sacrifice for each protégé who enters this two-year intensive experience. What I underestimated was the enormous commitment it would require from me. By selecting them, I was choosing to make a significant investment in their life, from the beginning to the end of the experience. And just as with Teach For America, our team at Mosaic focuses on what type of person we're selecting with extreme care because we have limited spots and we desire to maximize the investments we're making. This is what drives me to pray fervently for wisdom in the selection process. Although I can't tell you every quality that Jesus used to select His disciples, I have made observations from the Gospels and developed my own list of qualities to look for in selecting where to give my efforts of leadership investment.

I don't know the exact context you're in, but if you want to improve your process in selecting whom to mentor, whom to recruit onto your team, which staff member or volunteer to give your best time to, or in whom to invest in some other way, here are six characteristics (which I've extracted from the Gospels) that I look for in assessing who is a true investor:

1. Generative: They willingly serve others with a positive attitude of love and helpfulness, as they generate good. They consistently maintain a generative spirit as they strive to love others well. They embody what Jesus embodies—they live to serve, not to be served. Translated another way, they seek to give, not to take. They unselfishly offer their time for other people who in turn unselfishly give their time away for still others. And when necessary, they sacrifice for others with authentic, selfless love.

2. Grateful: They value people's time and resources and even express it. Thank-you is part of their regular vocabulary. They see every ounce of investment that a person gives them as an undeserved gift. They don't demand anything, and what others give is always more than enough.

3. Teachable: They sustain a consistent humble posture, and a strong desire to grow. It's not just that they want to learn knowledge; they open up their lives to learning from people through relationship, and their learning changes them. They are humble enough to receive advice, suggestions, and input from others.

4. Missional: They live with conviction for their mission. They believe they have a calling, a significant contribution to make, and that something must be done to bring change in the world. They are focused and driven to pursue the cause they believe in.

5. Strategic: They think wisely and intentionally about how to use their time well, rather than being casual or even flippant with how they spend it. They strive to expend their best efforts on people who can multiply their impact and advance their mission.

6. Resilient: They are able to keep going when the going gets tough. Giving up is not an option. They realize that in order to accomplish their mission they must push through obstacles and challenges that hinder progress and forward movement. We want to invest in people who are going to be successful, and successful people don't give up when it's hard.

Whatever your leadership context, one of the most relationally intelligent decisions you can make is selecting who you invest in. There is enormous gravity to your selection, and it begins by improving your ability to spot investors. It continues in the quality of your investment in those you've selected. If you invest in a person who doesn't invest in others, you have an impact on only one person. But if you invest in those who will receive it, apply it, and then reinvest in others, your impact grows disproportionately. This leaves behind a legacy that you can't leave by investing in takers. When you do this right, you'll begin seeing disproportionate influence throughout your life.

Quality Versus Quantity

As you move forward in your relational investments, one thing is for sure: it's not as much about how many people you invest in, but way more about the quality of your investment. At the core of relational intelligence is cultivating healthy, quality relationships. Relational geniuses know how to engage with others through intelligence, intentionality, and authentic love that strives to serves others more than self. It's better to invest in a few who will reinvest in others, than to invest in many who may never reinvest in anyone. In other words, it's more important to do less with quantity and focus more on quality. Then people around you will do the same as they emulate your leadership example. This is the way of a relational genius and a new way of being smart.

> It's better to invest in a few who will reinvest in others than to invest in many who may never reinvest in anyone.

9

The Last Word

When Jesus walked among us, He elevated the necessity of healthy, quality relationships. He declared that the most important value in life revolves around how well we as human beings relate to one another in love. He knew that love is what ultimately transforms people, communities, and the world as we know it. At the same time, He knew that simply believing in love didn't change anything—and that's where so many of us often find ourselves, stuck in the belief of love rather than advancing the movement of love. The journey through this book has been about learning how to move from belief to action as we engage our relationships through *a new way of being smart*. Relational intelligence is about living out love with one eye on influence, but always remembering to keep it in right order—love first, influence second. It not only works better that way, but it's also the right way to lead. It's the way we as leaders serve humanity and God Himself, while also creating a distinct and better world. Hopefully, *Relational Intelligence* has reinforced your value to do relationships well and helped equip you to carry out this mission.

Notes

1: The Human Economy
1. John 13:34–35, NIV.

2: The Michael Scott Syndrome
1. Matt. 7:3–5, NIV.
2. Assaya, M. *Bono in Conversation*. New York: Riverhead Books, 2005, p. 85.
3. George, B., Sims, P., McLean, A. N., and Mayer, D. "Discovering Your Authentic Leadership." *Harvard Business Review*, Feb. 2007, p. 133.

Part 2: The Hidden Power of a Relational Genius
1. Collins, B. *When in Doubt, Tell the Truth: And Other Quotations from Mark Twain*. New York: Columbia University Press, 1997.

3: The Story Collector
1. Migel, P. *Titania: The Biography of Isak Dinesen*. New York: Random House, 1967.
2. Philippians 2:3–4, NIV.
3. Lencioni, P. *Three Signs of a Miserable Job*. San Francisco: Jossey-Bass, 2007.

4: The Energy Carrier
1. Mark 12:28–34, NASB.

5: The Compelling Relator

1. Emerson, R. W. *Hitch Your Wagon to a Star and Other Quotations from Ralph Waldo Emerson*. New York: Columbia University Press, 1996.
2. Extracted from a conversation with Mark Kvamme (a venture capitalist and employee at Sequoia Capital).
3. Godin, S. *Tribes: We Need You to Lead Us*. London: Penguin Books, 2008.
4. Luke 6:26, TNIV.
5. John 4:1–21, TNIV.
6. Ibid.

6: The Conversational Futurist

1. John 3:1–15, NIV.
2. Matt. 16:2–4, TNIV.
3. John 8:1–11, NIV.

7: The Likeable Hero

1. Smith, G. P. *Here Today Here Tomorrow: Transforming Your Workforce from High Turnover to High Retention*. Chicago: Dearborn Financial Publishing, 2001.
2. Lencioni, P. *Three Signs of a Miserable Job*. San Francisco: Jossey-Bass, 2007.

8: The Disproportionate Investor

1. Wilgoren, J. "Wendy Kopp, Leader of Teach For America." *New York Times*, Nov. 12, 2000.
2. Luke 9:24, NIV.
3. Haggai 1:5b–6, NIV.
4. Matt. 25:14–30, *The Message*.

Bibliography

Assayas, Michka. *Bono: In Conversation with Michka Assayas*. New York: Penguin Group, 2006.

Brafman, Ori, and Rod A. Beckstrom. *The Spider and the Starfish*. New York: Penguin Group, 2006.

Bryant, Eric. *Peppermint Filled Piñatas*. Grand Rapids, Mich.: Zondervan, 2006.

Buckingham, Marcus, and Curt Coffman. *First Break All the Rules*. New York: Simon & Schuster, 1999.

Buckingham, Marcus, and Donald O. Clifton. *Now Discover Your Strengths*. New York: Free Press, 2001.

Cloud, Henry. *Boundaries*. Grand Rapids, Mich.: Zondervan, 1992.

Cloud, Henry, and John Townsend. *Safe People*. Grand Rapids, Mich.: Zondervan, 1995.

Cloud, Henry, and John Townsend. *How People Grow*. Grand Rapids, Mich.: Zondervan, 2001.

Godin, Seth. *Tribes*. New York: Penguin Group, 2008.

Goleman, Daniel. *Working with Emotional Intelligence*. New York: Bantam Books, 1998.

Goleman, Daniel, Annie McKee, and Richard E Boyatzis. *Primal Leadership*. Boston: Harvard Business School, 2002.

Heath, Chip, and Dan Heath. *Made to Stick*. New York: Random House, 2007.

Keirsey, David. *Please Understand Me II*. Del Mar, Calif.: Prometheus Nemesis, 1998.

Kouzes, James M., and Barry C. Posner. *The Leadership Challenge*. San Francisco: Jossey-Bass, 2007.

Loehr, Jim, and Tony Schwartz. *The Power of Full Engagement*. New York: Free Press, 2002.

Lencioni, Patrick. *The Five Dysfunctions of a Team*. San Francisco: Jossey-Bass, 2002.

Lencioni, Patrick. *Death by Meeting*. San Francisco: Jossey-Bass, 2004.

McManus, Erwin. *Chasing Daylight*. Nashville: Thomas Nelson, 2002.

McManus, Erwin. *Uprising*. Nashville: Thomas Nelson, 2006.

Myers, Isabel. *Gifts Differing: Understanding Personality Types*. Mountain View, Calif.: Davis-Black, 1995.

Ortberg, John. *Everyone's Normal Until You Get to Know Them*. Grand Rapids, Mich.: Zondervan, 2003.

Ortberg, John. *The Me I Want to Be*. Grand Rapids, Mich.: Zondervan, 2009.

Palmer, Stephanie. *Good in a Room*. New York: Doubleday, 2008.

Pink, Daniel H. *A Whole New Mind*. New York: Penguin Group, 2005.

Quenk, Naomi L. *Essentials of Myers-Briggs Type Indicator Assessment*. Hoboken, N.J.: Wiley, 2000.

Rath, Tom. *Strengths Finder 2.0*. New York: Gallup Press, 2007.

Sanders, Tim. *Love Is a Killer App*. New York: Random House, 2002.

Sanders, Tim. *The Likeability Factor*. New York: Random House, 2005.

Scazzero, Peter. *Emotionally Healthy Spirituality*. Nashville: Thomas Nelson, 2006.

Scazzero, Peter, and Warren Bird. *Emotionally Healthy Church*. Grand Rapids, Mich.: Zondervan, 2003.

Seligman, Martin E. P. *Learned Optimism: How to Change Your Mind and Your Life*. New York: Knopf, 1991.

Stanley, Andy. *It Came from Within: The Shocking Truth of What Lies in the Heart*. Sisters, Ore.: Multnomah, 2006.

Townsend, John. *Loving People: How to Love and Be Loved*. Nashville: Thomas Nelson, 2007.

The Author

Steve Saccone serves as a Catalyst at Mosaic, a community of faith in Los Angeles. He continues to be a pioneer in leadership development, as he founded and currently leads Protégé, a two-year global leadership program designed for future entrepreneurs, church planters, and spiritual leaders. In addition, he works as a Faith Field Advisor for the Gallup Organization and as a consultant for *Monvee*, as well as serving as a Gallup Strengths Performance Coach. He has a master's degree in transformational leadership from Bethel Seminary and lives in Los Angeles with his wife, Cheri, and son, Hudson.

Index

Reverse Mentoring

How Young Leaders Can Transform the Church and Why We Should Let Them

EARL CREPS

Hardcover | ISBN: 978-0-470-18898-9

"The world has ended about four times. New technologies and processes for handling information make the old world obsolete, quickly. When this happens an unusual dynamic asserts itself. Younglings mentor the elders into the way of the new world. The richness of life sharing that is established in reverse mentoring is a largely unexplored, but promising green edge to the Christian movement. Let Earl Creps show you how to get in on this development."

—Reggie McNeal, author, *Missional Renaissance* and *The Present Future*

In this groundbreaking book, Earl Creps addresses how older ministry leaders can learn from younger peers who are in closer touch with today's culture, technology, and social climate. He reveals the practical benefits of reverse mentoring and offers down-to-earth steps for implementing it at both the personal and the organizational level.

Reverse Mentoring offers a guide for leaders who want to experience personal formation by exercising the kind of humility that invites a younger person to become a tutor. Earl Creps details specific benefits of reverse mentoring in areas such as evangelism, communication, and leadership, clearly showing how to develop healthy reverse mentoring relationships that will garner positive results.

Reverse Mentoring is a model for church leaders who understand the importance of learning from younger people to prevent functional obsolescence and to transform their leadership and mission.

EARL CREPS has been a pastor, ministries consultant, and university professor. Along the way, Creps earned a Ph.D. in communication at Northwestern University and a doctor of ministry degree in leadership at AGTS. He is the author of *Off-Road Disciplines* from Jossey-Bass.

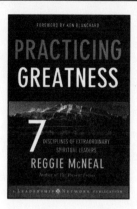

Practicing Greatness
7 Disciplines of Extraordinary Spiritual Leaders

REGGIE MCNEAL
FOREWORD BY KEN BLANCHARD

Hardcover | ISBN: 978-0-7879-7753-5

"The depth and breadth of wisdom in this book is just short of unbelievable. Good leaders aspiring to be great leaders will do well to read this book and allow it to probe and shape their lives."

—**Bill Easum,** Easum, Bandy & Associates

How do good spiritual leaders become great leaders?

Based on his experience coaching and mentoring thousands of Christian leaders across a broad spectrum of ministry settings, bestselling leadership expert and consultant Reggie McNeal helps spiritual leaders understand that they will self-select into or out of greatness.

In this important book, McNeal shows how great spiritual leaders are committed consciously and intentionally to seven spiritual disciplines, habits of heart and mind that shape both their character and competence.

Practicing Greatness goes beyond mere clichés and inspirational thoughts to be a hard-hitting resource for leaders who aspire to go from being just good enough to being great leaders who bless others.

REGGIE MCNEAL is the director of leadership development for the South Carolina Baptist Convention. Through his extensive coaching roles, he has been devoted to helping leaders understand and practice true leadership greatness. Mr. McNeal is the author of *Revolution in Leadership: Training Apostles for Tomorrow's Church, A Work of Heart: Understanding How God Shapes Spiritual Leaders* and the best-selling *The Present Future: Six Tough Questions for the Church.*

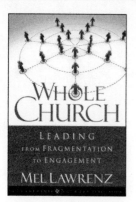

Whole Church

Leading from Fragmentation to Engagement

MEL LAWRENZ

Hardcover | ISBN: 978-0-470-25934-4

"Mel is a thoughtful analyst of church life today. Best of all—he actually does what he writes about. This book can lead to new levels of engagement for your church." —John Ortberg, author and pastor, Menlo Park Presbyterian Church

In this timely book Mel Lawrenz—pastor of one of the most innovative churches in America—outlines his proven model for "whole church/whole ministry." Church leaders and congregants can embrace this model to reinvigorate their mission by engaging with God, each other, their community, and the world. A "whole church" means that a local congregation believes it is called to the whole purpose of God in and through the church, rather than some narrowly defined specialization.

As Lawrenz explains, all too often the church talks about God's great provisions (grace, salvation, mercy), but they are not applied in real and practical ways in people's lives. As a result many Christians have become disengaged. Step by step, Lawrenz shows how to apply the four types of engagement that will integrate a church.

The dynamic whole church model is not merely a list of functions or stages of growth. It offers practical, down-to-earth ways to connect the church to its true mission and purpose.

MEL LAWRENZ is senior pastor at Elmbrook Church in Brookfield, Wisconsin. His Internet ministry, The Brook (www.ComeToTheBrook.org), offers text, audio, and video content to a general audience and to church leaders. Lawrenz is also the host of a weekly regional radio interview program, Faith Conversations, and is the author of several books.